£5.95

Schools History Project 13–16

Energy consultant and historical researcher: Hugh Miall

Project editor: Denis Shemilt
Trinity and All Saints' College, Leeds

ENERGY THROUGH TIME
Joe Scott

D1081391

This book is to be returned on or before
the last date stamped

D1081392

Oxford University Press

Oxford University Press, Walton Street, Oxford OX2 6DP

Oxford New York Toronto
Petaling Jaya Singapore Hong Kong Tokyo
Delhi Bombay Calcutta Madras Karachi
Nairobi Dar es Salaam Cape Town
Melbourne Auckland

and associated companies in
Beirut Berlin Ibadan Nicosia

Oxford is a trade mark of Oxford University Press

First published 1986
Reprinted 1987

ISBN 0 19 913304 2

Typeset by Oxford Publishing Services, Oxford
Printed in Hong Kong

Illustrations by Peter Bailey,
Peter Connolly, John Ireland, Oxford
Illustrators, Bernard Robinson and
Mike Saunders.

Schools History Project 13–16

This project was set up by the Schools
Council in 1972. Its main aim was to
suggest suitable objectives for history
teachers, and to promote the use of
appropriate materials and teaching
methods for their realisation. This involved
a reconsideration of the nature of history
and its relevance in secondary schools; the
design of a syllabus framework which
shows the uses that history may have in the
education of adolescents; and the setting
up of appropriate examinations.

The project received a boost in 1984
when additional funding was provided in
SCDC to finance the revision of existing
materials.

Since 1978 the project has been based
at Trinity and All Saint's College, Leeds,
where it is one of three national curriculum
development projects run and supported
by the Centre for History Education.

The material has been produced with the
help of a financial contribution from the
Department of Energy, but does not
necessarily reflect its views.

Enquiries about the project should be
addressed to:

Ian Dawson, Director of SHP 13–16
Trinity and All Saints College
Brownberrie Lane,
Horsforth,
Leeds LS18 5HD

Foreword

This book addresses crucial and fundamental questions about how and why things happen in human affairs. Although History has no solutions to offer to the problems and complexities of the contemporary world, it is vital to the social and political education of young people that they understand some of the problems faced by their predecessors, the reasons for actions taken and the consequences that have followed.

The Schools History Project 13 – 16 and, in particular, the Studies in Development are intended to help pupils to understand the processes of *change* and *cause* in history and thereby,

a) to come to terms with 'the tragedy of good intentions' in human history, and to realise that, in part, the ills and disappointments of the modern world follow from well intentioned and sometimes heroic attempts to set things right. They should also appreciate that, but for the heroism and unremitting endeavour of predecessors, the world in which we live would be a deal less comfortable, secure and just than it is;

b) to grasp the nature and limits of individual and collective action in human affairs. Although people possess considerable freedom to select goals and initiate actions, they are far less free to control and limit the consequences of actions;

c) to understand how past, present and future are related. The future is not determined but future possibilities are determinate. What can be made to happen is limited by what has already happened and is now happening. But the past does not provide a model for what is possible or desirable in the future.

The topic of *Energy through Time* has been selected for three reasons. First, because it is a useful vehicle for teaching transferable ideas about change and cause in human affairs. Second, because world and domestic energy policies are important issues in their own right. The future health, wealth and happiness of adolescents is intimately bound up with decisions about energy conservation, distribution and technology. Third, the study of *Energy through Time* may be used to teach economic literacy, awareness of 'the world of work' and understanding of technological change. As such, the topic may serve to reinforce and complement TVEI type courses, albeit within the framework of a broad and balanced liberal curriculum. It may also facilitate a measure of continuity between GCSE and CPVE courses, particularly if the latter contain a significant fraction of industrial and/or economic history.

A Teacher's Guide is published to accompany *Energy through Time*. It explains the design of the book and makes detailed suggestions for its use in relation to the Schools History Project.

Sources throughout the book have been adapted for the use of pupils of 14 – 16. Sentences have been shortened, spellings modernised or modern words substituted, and no attempt has been made to indicate elisions or omissions.

Project Editor   DENIS SHEMILT

Contents

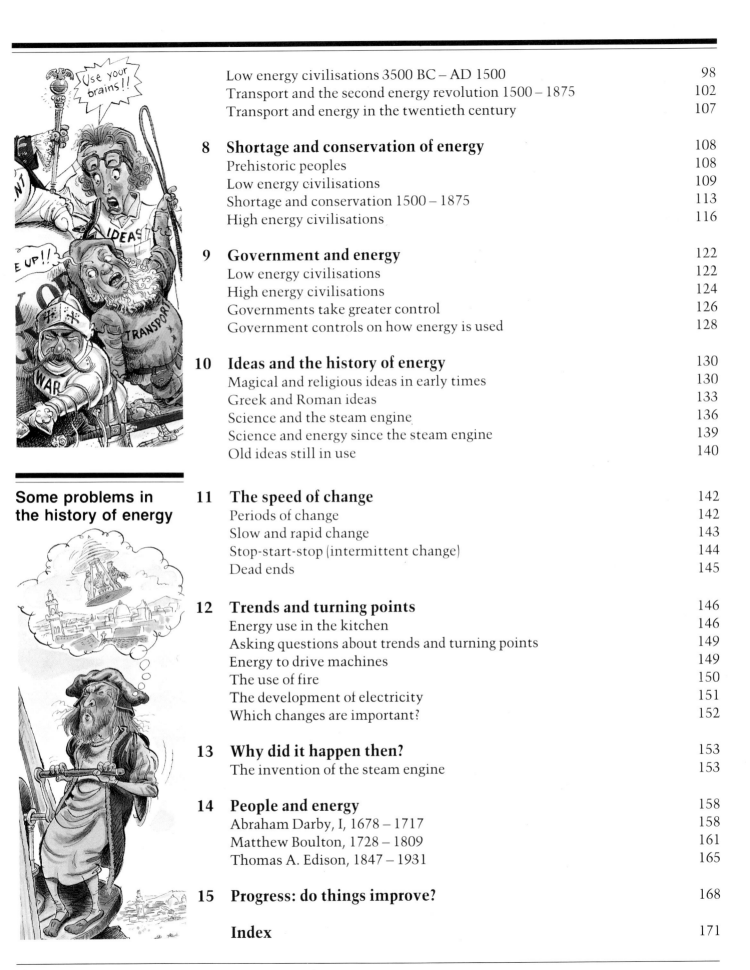

Acknowledgements

The publishers would like to thank the following for permission to use photos:
Acurex, p. 144; All-sport, p. 140; Atlas Copco (Great Britain) Ltd, p. 71 (centre right); Barnaby's Picture Library, p. 25 (centre); BBC Hulton Picture Library, pp. 40, 42, 48, 62 (top), 75 (bottom) and 98; Bayerische Staatsbibliothek, Munich, p. 32; Bibliothèque Nationale, Paris, p. 114; Bilderdienst Süddeutscher Verlag, p. 125; Bodleian Library, Oxford, p. 34 (bottom); Bridgeman Art Library, p. 36 (bottom); British Ceramic Research Association Ltd., p. 128 (both); British Gas, p. 73 (top and bottom right); British Library, London, pp. 8 (top), 29, 30 (top), 34 (top left), 92 (bottom), 94 and 135; British Museum, p. 19; British Petroleum, p. 68 (centre); Camerapix Hutchinson Library, pp. 18 (bottom) and 108; Camera Press, p. 80; Central Electricity Generating Board, p. 151; Christ Church, Oxford, p. 30 (bottom); Daily Telegraph, p. 81 (bottom left); Department of Special Collections Library, University of California, Santa Barbara, p. 117; Drake Well Museum, Pennsylvania, p. 66 (both); Earthscan, pp. 8 (middle), 12, 86 (all) 97; E T Archive, p. 54 (top); Fiat Auto (UK) Ltd., p. 81 (top right); Ford Motor Co. Ltd., p. 71 (top left); Henry Ford Museum, The Edison Institute, Dearborn, Michigan, pp. 165 (both) and 167; Fotomas, p. 55 (top right); Giraudon, pp. 36 (top), 92 (top left and centre); Grove Coles, p. 71 (centre left); Robert Harding, pp. 31 (top right), 91 (bottom left), 92 (top right), 110, 130 (both) and 168 (left); Helmshore Museum of the Lancashire Textile Industry, p. 53; Michael Holford, pp. 18 (top), 23, 24 (top and bottom), 27, 31, 90, 91 (top) and 147 (bottom); Holkham Hall, Norfolk, p. 34 (top right); Illustrated London News, p. 51 (top); Imperial War Museum, London, p. 72 (centre); Ironbridge Gorge Museum Trust (Elton Collection), pp. 154, 159, 160; Itaipu Binacional, Brazil, p. 120 (top); William Lee Ltd (photo: Geoffrey B. Platts) p. 81 (top left); Leeds Postcards, p. 78 (top); J K Major, pp. 93 (top and centre), 106 and 163; Manchester Central Library, p. 78 (bottom); Mansell Collection, pp. 20, 25 (top) and 93 (bottom); Mary Evans Picture Library, pp. 52 (top, and bottom), 54 (bottom), 58 (bottom), 64 (right) and 67; Massey-Ferguson, p. 71 (bottom left); Mercedes-Benz (UK) Ltd, p. 143 (bottom); Metropolitan Museum of Art, New York, p. 14 (top); NASA, p. 136, National Maritime Museum, Greenwich, pp. 102 and 113; National Motor Museum, Beaulieu, p. 70 (bottom); Oakland Museum, California, p. 105; Pan Am, p. 72 (bottom); Perkins Engines 71 (centre); Philips Petroleum p. 69; Popperfoto, pp. 75 (middle) and 85; Primesight, p. 71 (bottom right); Royal Collection, Windsor Castle. Reproduced by Gracious Permission of Her Majesty the Queen, p. 161 (top); Scala, p. 99; Science Museum, London, pp. 38, 45, 63, 133 and 156; Shell Photographic Service, p. 68 (top and bottom); Spectrum, p. 111 (top); Sutcliffe Gallery, Whitby, p. 103; Jeffrey Tabberner, p. 62 (bottom); Tate Gallery, London, p. 161 (bottom); Taylor Woodrow, p. 120 (bottom left); Ullstein Bilderdienst, p. 50; United Kingdom Atomic Energy Authority pp. 76, 120 (bottom right); United States Information Service, p. 127; Vosper Thornycroft, p. 71 (top right); Weidenfeld and Nicolson, pp. 51 (bottom) and 99 (bottom); Zefa, pp. 74, 81 (bottom right) and 121 (both).

Line illustrations are reproduced mostly from Singer: *A History of Technology*, Vols I–VII (OUP).

Introduction

Once, before the discovery of fire, human beings, like other animals, could only use the energy of their own muscles. Today, in a rich country like Britain we use many other sources of energy as well.

■ *How many sources of energy can you think of?*

In this book the word 'energy' is used to mean this extra fuel and power. Some of it we use directly to keep warm and to cook our food. Some of it we use indirectly to run machines to do work for us. In 1981 each person in Britain used, on average, the amount of energy there is in five tonnes of coal, although it was used in other forms like petrol or electricity as well as coal.

■ *What would life be like if we had little or no extra energy to make use of?*

In Britain today we each use a great deal of energy, much of it by means of machines. How many machines can you spot in this picture?

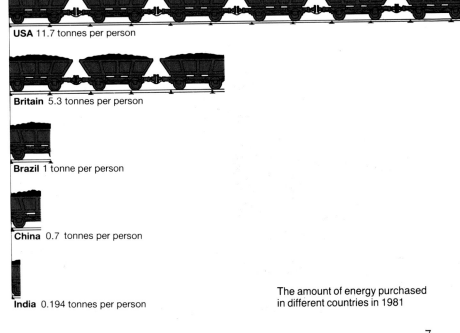

USA 11.7 tonnes per person

Britain 5.3 tonnes per person

Brazil 1 tonne per person

China 0.7 tonnes per person

India 0.194 tonnes per person

The amount of energy purchased in different countries in 1981

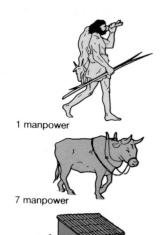

1 manpower

7 manpower

30 manpower

13 million manpower

Through time people have made animals and machines work for them

Each person in Britain today has at least 85 'energy slaves'

Source 1 Ploughing in England, early fourteenth century. An illustration from a Bible

Source 2 Ploughing in the Wollo region of Ethiopia

In 1981 the average Indian bought only the amount of energy there is in 194 kilograms of coal. This does not count the firewood they collected for themselves, but even taking that into account, the Indians are much poorer in energy than the British. We would have to go back 300 years to find a time when there was as little energy available per person in Britain.

A very few people today, like the bushmen of the Kalahari, still use no extra energy except for a little firewood.

But they do know how to control fire, unlike the earliest human beings.

This book is about the development of human use of energy from the early people who discovered fire to us with our nuclear power stations. It is about the way in which human beings made animals or machines work for them.

We use many different sorts of energy in modern Britain. About half of it is wasted. If we add the rest together and divide by the total population, we can work out how much there is for each of us. It works out that there is 85 times as much as one human being could produce working steadily eight hours a day. There are 85 'energy slaves' at the command of the average person living in Britain today.

- *What were the main stages in this movement from the early man-like creatures who commanded no 'energy slaves' to us with 85 each?*

- *Did these changes happen evenly all the time or in sudden jerks?*

- *Why did they happen when they did?*

- *We have seen already that some areas lag behind today. Why did some areas take the lead at some periods and lag behind at others?*

THE STORY OF ENERGY THROUGH TIME

This history of human use of energy begins half a million years ago with man's first use of fire. It comes down to the present day, so it includes many changes like the coming of nuclear power which are still going on. To help to make sense of this long story the book refers to three periods of time.

The first of these periods, the Old Stone Age, was by far the longest. The most recent, the period of 'high energy civilisation' in which we live, has only lasted so far for about 100 years.

The changes that ended the Old Stone Age, and the changes that brought about our modern civilisation are so important in the history of energy that we can call them 'energy revolutions'. The first of them began when people discovered farming and learned to live together in large permanent settlements. They had new needs for energy and new ways of getting it, and thus brought about what we can call 'low energy civilisations'. The second 'energy revolution' took place when people began to use machines like the steam engine at mines, in factories and for transport. Again new needs for energy and new ways of getting it led to great changes, and brought in the 'high energy civilisation' of today.

1 Fire and the hunter

Source 3 *Above:* A cast of the skull of Peking Man (*Homo Erectus*) with (*below*) a drawing of his head based on the skull

An antler tip hardened in the fire, found at Choukoutien

For most of human history people have lived by hunting, moving from place to place to follow the herds of wild animals. When they moved they had to carry everything with them, so their techniques and their tools were simple. People like us ('homo sapiens') appeared over 100000 years ago, but long before that our ancestors ('homo erectus') had learned how to make stone tools and weapons – the first technology. And they had learned how to make fire – the first use of energy.

Some of our earliest evidence of human control of fire comes from the Choukoutien cave, near Peking. The owner of this skull lived in the cave about 500000 years ago. His brain was only about two thirds as big as ours, but he was clever enough to make tools and to use fire. People like him used the cave for about 300000 years.

Source 4 Evidence of fire
One of the most important discoveries in the cave was the first clear evidence of the use of fire by hominids. This appeared even in the earliest time of occupation. Thick layers of ash, burned and charred bone, all restricted to what were quite unmistakably hearths, were found in several parts of the cave. Peking Man clearly retreated to the shelter of the cave during the cold winter months, keeping himself warm and other animals at bay by the flames of a fire. The cavern was big enough for a band of twenty or so, and they appear to have returned to the cave year after year. One of the ash layers is six metres thick.
(Richard E. Leakey: *The Making of Mankind* 1981)

An artist's idea of a group of cave dwellers at about 20000 BC, towards the end of the Old Stone Age

How was fire discovered?

There are plenty of natural fires, caused by lightning or volcanoes. The sun's heat and the friction of dry branches rubbing together in the wind can cause fire. But there is no evidence to tell us how Peking Man, or one of his ancestors, found how to make and use fire.

- *Is fire likely to have been discovered just once, by one person who taught everyone else? Or is it likely to have been discovered over and over again at different places and times?*

Why was fire important?

Fire made an enormous difference to human life. Cooking made meat much easier to eat (especially for the young and the old). It also stopped it going bad so quickly. Fire could be used to harden and to shape wood and bone tools.

Fire also made it possible for people to live in the colder northern regions and to stay there during the ice ages, which ended only about 10 000 years ago. So human beings spread to almost every part of the world.

Fire must also have changed people's ideas. To the stone age hunters themselves it must have seemed something more than a useful tool. As they relaxed, ate together, danced and laughed in the firelight, safe within the fire's magic circle of warmth and light, they knew it as something which held the whole life of their group together. Perhaps they saw fire as a god who must be served and fed, who could eat up whole forests or leave people to shiver and die if they failed to treat him properly. We have little evidence of how they thought and felt, but sometimes the skeletons of dead members of the group have been found buried near the hearth. It looks as if they were trying to keep the family together by the fire-side, even in the face of death. Ideas connecting the family with hearths and fire-sides are still strong.

- *What other sorts of evidence might there be about the ideas and feelings of these early users of fire?*

Fire causes new problems

As soon as people moved into regions too cold to live without fire, they were faced with two new problems – how to keep the fire alive, and how to light a new one if it went out. Perhaps the layer of ash six metres thick at Choukoutien (see Source 4) is evidence that the Peking people kept their fire burning all the time. But all our real evidence about people doing this comes from much later times.

Source 5 Keeping a spark of fire

Odysseus covered himself with leaves, just like a farmer in a lonely farmstead in the hills who hides away a glowing piece of wood in the black ashes, so as to keep his fire alive and save having to go off a long way to fetch a light.
(Homer: *The Odyssey*, Greece, C.700 BC.)

It must have been far more difficult for nomadic hunters to keep fire alive than for settled Greek farmers. Again we have no evidence.

- *What methods could the nomads use?*

It is far harder to light a new fire than to keep an old one going. Some fire-lighting tools were probably invented during the Old Stone Age, but they were made of perishable material and have left us no evidence. But there is plenty of evidence of the fire-lighting tools used by primitive people in recent times.

- *Is it safe to say that tools like these must have been invented in the Old Stone Age?*

- *Which of them is likely to have been invented first?*

For over 400 000 years the hunters of the Old Stone Age used fire in much the same way as 'homo erectus' had used it at Choukoutien. Their tools improved and they became more skilful hunters, but their use of energy remained much the same. Then, about 10 000 years ago, came the first farmers, with a new way of life, and new ways of using energy.

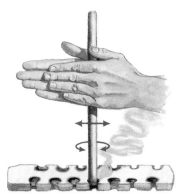

African fire-drill, twentieth century

Fire-plough, Pacific islands, twentieth century

Inuit bow-drill, Arctic, twentieth century

Tinder of dried moss or fungus

Percussion method, Neolithic age

Fire lighting tools

The first energy revolution

People carrying firewood home to a modern village in Niger

Right: The earliest farming settlements

Source 6 The skull of an early Jericho villager, about 6000 BC. His face has been reconstructed in plaster with cowrie shells for eyes

New uses for fire

The first farmers

Life in Jericho was quite different from the life of the nomadic hunters of the Old Stone Age. About 10000 years ago, as the last ice age was ending, the people of this area learned how to farm. They were probably the first farmers in the world. They had a steady food supply and could stay permanently in the same place. There has been a village or town at Jericho ever since.

Fuel supply in the farming village

The settled farmers of Jericho could produce and store a surplus of food. So more children and old people survived

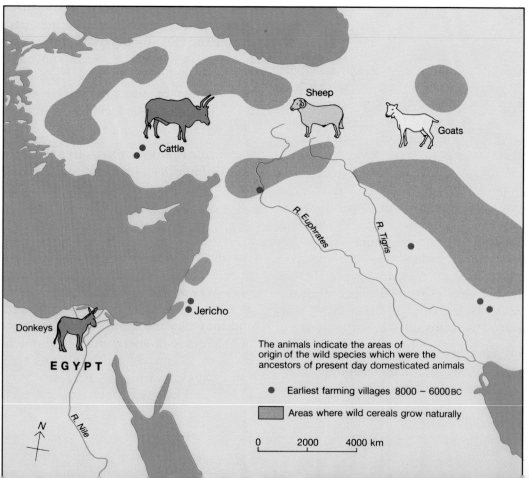

Cattle

Sheep

Goats

R. Euphrates

R. Tigris

Jericho

Donkeys

EGYPT

R. Nile

The animals indicate the areas of origin of the wild species which were the ancestors of present day domesticated animals

● Earliest farming villages 8000 – 6000 BC

▨ Areas where wild cereals grow naturally

0   2000   4000 km

N

and the population rose. By 7000BC there were about 2000 people at Jericho, all needing a steady supply of fuel for cooking and for warmth in winter. The nomadic hunters of the Old Stone Age had moved about in bands of about 20 people over hunting grounds which might be 10 or 20 kilometres across. So they could easily find wood to burn whenever they wanted. It grew much faster than they used it up.

Now things were different. People had to go out of the village to fetch back their fire-wood. As the village grew, they had further to go.

- *If more land was used for crops, how would that effect the fuel supply?*

- *If flocks of goats and sheep ate the seedlings of bushes and trees, what effect would that have?*

There is not much evidence about fuel supply in the villages of the early farmers.

Pottery: fire used to make things
Old Stone Age hunters used fire to cook, to keep warm and to harden wood or bone tools. New Stone Age farmers used fire to make things. Pottery was the first industry which was based on the use of energy.

The very earliest layer at Jericho has no pottery, but pots are found in all the later layers. In other neolithic sites all over the world there is almost always pottery.

Pottery does not decay, but the early kilns in which it was made have disappeared without trace. Crude pots could be fired in the open, piled together with brushwood. A specially constructed kiln could reach a higher temperature and make better pots. But a kiln needed a steady supply of wood.

- *What effect would pottery have on the fuel problem?*

- *Why should farming people think pottery so important?*

- *Why did nomadic hunters have no pottery?*

Source 7 *Above*: A neolithic pot from northern India, about 2500 BC. *Left*: A neolithic pot from China, about 4000 BC. The drawing of the face is the only one known on neolithic pottery

This is what an early kiln might have looked like

Walls of baked clay

Pots

Grate of baked clay supported in the middle

Animals: a new source of energy

a

b

c

Source 8 These paintings from an Egyptian tomb were made about 1400 BC, thousands of years after the development of farming. But they show the work that had to be done by all early farmers

a) Hoeing, breaking clods and sowing seeds
b) Reaping corn
c) Winnowing, to separate the wheat from the chaff

There was plenty of hard work on a neolithic farm. Life in the farming village may have been safer than the life of a hunter, though less exciting. But it meant far more hard, continuous, back-breaking work.

As well as bringing new sorts of work, farming brough a new source of energy. As soon as the early farmers had tamed animals, they might begin to use them to help with the work. It was a development in the history of energy as important as the first use of fire to make things.

When were animals first used to work for man?

1 The bones of domesticated cattle are smaller than wild ones.

■ *Why should the early farmers have tamed the smaller cattle?*

The smaller bones are found at many neolithic sites from about 6000 BC onwards.

2 There are plenty of Egyptian pictures of animals at work but none from earlier than 3000 BC.

■ *If methods like those at the top of page 15 were used by earlier farmers, would archaeologists find evidence of it?*

3 The plough is one of the most important energy-using tools in history. When animals could be harnessed to pull a plough, men and women needed

no longer to do the back-breaking work of hoeing and digging. Again, the earliest pictures come from Egypt.

Source 9 A hand mill or quern for grinding corn, from Jericho. The corn is modern!

Source 10 An Egyptian tomb model, about 2500 BC, which shows how the quern was used

Source 11 Egyptian tomb carvings, about 2500 BC.

a) Goats treading in the seed.
b) Donkeys carrying home the corn.
c) Donkeys threshing (separating the grain from the straw) by treading the grain

a   b

c

Cattle have a convenient bony ridge on their shoulders. If a wooden bar, or yoke, is shaped to fit this ridge on two oxen, the plough can be fastened to it, and the oxen or cows can drag it along. Ox-yokes like this are still in use in many parts of the world. The ox-yoke was one of man's key inventions.

Source 12 Egyptian ploughs, from a tomb painting, about 1900 BC

- *What evidence would archaeologists be likely to find of ox-yokes or early ploughs?*

- *Which farming tasks would first be done by animals?*

- *When is it likely that ploughs were first used?*

Whenever animals were first put to work, it was an important stage in history. From that time until only 200 years ago animal power was to be man's only source of extra energy for land transport and for heavy work. Perhaps the fact that the Middle East had the right animals is one reason why it was there that civilisation first developed.

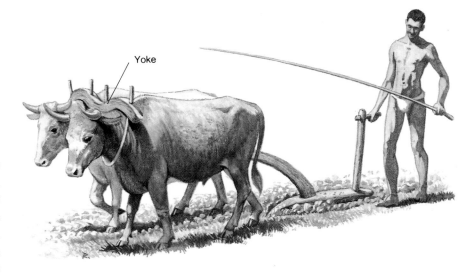

Yoke

This drawing shows how the yoke fitted to an early plough (about 4000 BC)

15

Changes and developments 8000–3500 BC

By 3500 BC there were farmers in only a few areas of the world. In these areas villages and even towns had been established, and the population was rising rapidly.

The early farmers had increased their use of fuel and had begun to transport it to their villages. They had begun to use it industrially to make pots. They were learning also how to make animals work for them.

The coming of farming had made these changes in energy use necessary. This 'Energy Revolution' was to continue, and to make it possible for some of these villages to grow into cities and empires – the first civilisations.

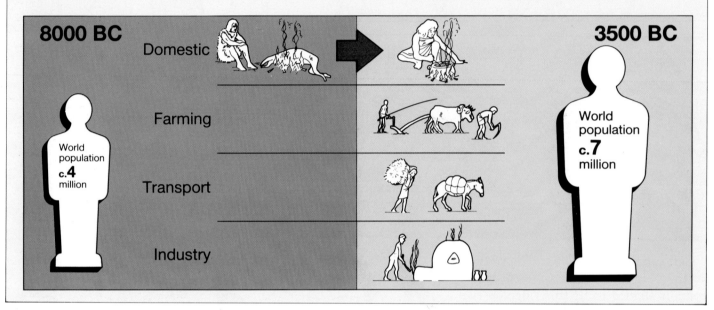

3 Low energy civilisations 3500 BC–AD 1500

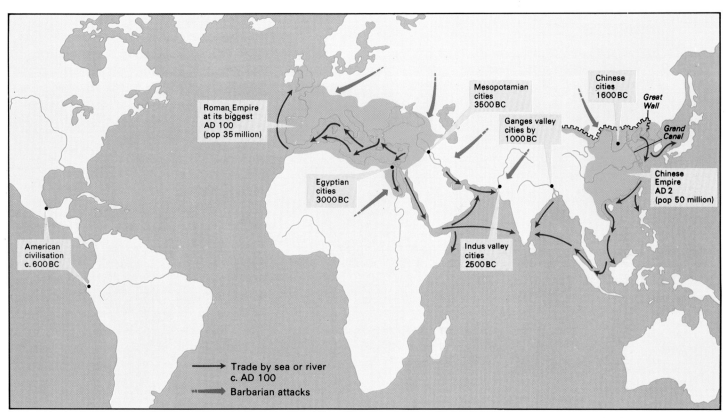

Early civilizations

Civilisation began about 3500BC. The first cities were in Mesopotamia, but others arose over the next 4000 years in Egypt, India, China, Greece and Rome and in Central America. In a city there was far more wealth and food to spare than in a village. Priests and teachers developed writing. Craftsmen built temples and palaces. Traders brought goods from far away. Emperors sent out armies to conquer other lands and cities.

■ *How did these changes affect the history of energy?*

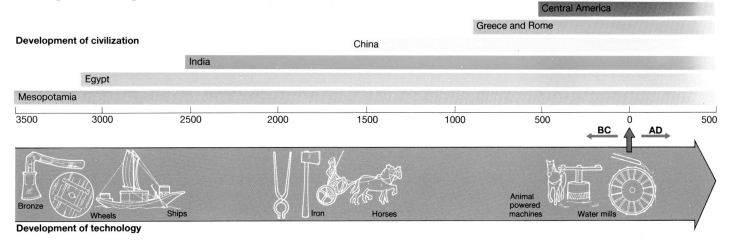

New needs for energy 3500 BC – AD 500

The early cities and empires needed much more energy than the farming villages of the neolithic period.

Fuel for the city

Many of the early cities were small by modern standards, but they were far bigger than the neolithic villages. At the time of the birth of Christ, Rome had a population of about one million. All these people had to cook and to keep warm in winter, so large amounts of fuel had to be brought into the city.

Fuel for metal working

Metals came into use at about the same time as civilisation began. Gold, silver and copper could be made into beautiful ornaments. Bronze and later iron made excellent tools and weapons. But to smelt copper or iron into useful metal required enormous amounts of fuel.

Energy for transport

Traders from the early cities travelled thousands of kilometres. Only expensive goods could be carried as far as that, but bulky goods, like wood or iron or corn had sometimes to be carried for hundreds of kilometres. The early city dwellers also needed a good supply of timber and stone for building. So it was important to develop improved methods of transport.

Energy for war

The civilised areas were a tempting target for attack. They had rich farmlands and cities. Wealthy merchants travelled with their goods by land and sea. On the edge of the civilised regions, semi-nomadic tribes lived by pastoral farming and robbery. If the Egyptians, or the Chinese, or the Romans were well organised and had better weapons than

Source 13 A bronze container used in religious ritual. It shows a tiger protecting a man, about 1300 BC

The Great Wall of China was built between 250 BC and AD 1650 to keep out nomadic raiders. It is 2400 km long

the nomads, they could keep them at bay, or even bring them under control. If the nomadic people had better weapons and organisation, they broke in and took what they wanted.

Energy for driving machines

In all the early civilisations most work was done by hand. In the towns craftsmen made things in small workshops. In the countryside most people were peasant farmers growing their own food and making cloth from the wool of their own sheep. So there was little need for machines. It was a 'non-mechanical' world. There were, however, a few important tasks which needed machines and energy to drive them. One of these was irrigation. The river valley civilisations of Mesopotamia, Egypt and China depended on irrigated farmland for their food. This usually meant that in the dry season water had to be raised from the river level so that it could flow on to the fields. A machine of some sort was needed to lift the water.

Machines were also needed in the mines from which the metal ores were dug. Water had to be lifted from flooded areas, and also the lumps of ore had to be crushed before being smelted.

In the city itself, heavy weights had to be lifted in building work, and large amounts of corn had to be ground into flour.

For most of the history of the early civilisations these tasks were performed by hand. But by about 500 BC people began to invent machines which needed sources of energy to power them.

Metal cooking pot and tripod

Charcoal fire

Source 15 A Roman hearth from Pompeii, Italy, AD 79

Source 14 Assyrian raising water from the river by 'shaduf'. The shaduf, on a mud upright, stood on the river bank, and in front a brick platform was built out into the river for the man who filled and emptied the bucket. A carving from the Palace at Nineveh, Mesopotamia, about 700 BC

1 Slavery

We do not know when slavery began. It was probably the result of tribal wars, since it was easy to make captured prisoners into slaves. But the stronger governments of the cities made slavery easier to organise, and it was quite common in the early civilisations.

Most people in Ancient Egypt or China or in the Roman Empire were not slaves. They were poor farmers growing their own crops. So as well as using slaves, governments often formed gangs of poor farmers and labourers to do work which needed large amounts of energy.

Source 18 Building the Pyramids

Cheops (to continue the account which the Egyptian priests gave me) compelled his subjects to labour as slaves. Some were forced to drag blocks of stone from the quarries in the Arabian hills to the Nile, where they were ferried across and taken over by others who hauled them to the Libyan hills. The work went on in three-monthly shifts, a hundred thousand men in a shift. To build the pyramid itself took twenty years; it is of polished stone blocks beautifully fitted, none of the blocks being less than ten metres long. An inscription is cut upon (the pyramid) in Egyptian characters recording the amount spent on radishes, onions and leeks for the labourers, and I remember distinctly that the interpreter who read me the inscription said the sum was 1600 talents of silver. If this is true, how much more must have been spent on bread and clothing for the labourers during all those years.
(Herodotus: *History*. Herodotus travelled to Egypt about 450 BC. Cheops' pyramid was built about 2550 BC)

■ *How reliable is Herodotus' account?*

Source 19 Grinding at the King's palace

The king's hand-mills stood in a building nearby. Twelve women had to toil away at these mills, grinding the barley and wheat into meal for the household bread.

When dawn broke they had all ground their share and gone off to sleep, except one not so vigorous as the rest who had not yet finished her task. This woman stopped her mill and said, 'Terrible work this, grinding meal for the young lords. They've broken my back. May this be their last dinner, say I.'
(Homer: *The Odyssey*, Greece c.700 BC.)

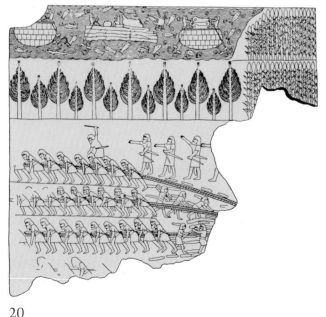

Source 16 Carving from a Roman tomb, about AD 100. A heavy stone carving being lifted by a treadmill crane

Source 17 Carving from the Assyrian Palace at Nineveh, Mesopotamia, about 700 BC. The massive statue of a bull is being dragged into position

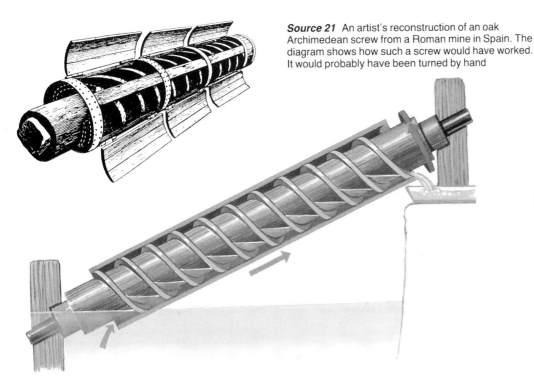

Source 21 An artist's reconstruction of an oak Archimedean screw from a Roman mine in Spain. The diagram shows how such a screw would have worked. It would probably have been turned by hand

Source 22 Slave working on an Archimedean screw. A pottery relief from Egypt, about AD 200

Source 23 Drawing published AD 1637 in China. But pedal pumps like this were the main Chinese method of raising water from at least 200 BC

Source 20 How the Romans tackled the water problem in the mines

As they go down deeper, they come upon underground rivers. What is most surprising of all is that they draw out the water by means of what is called the Egyptian screw. It was invented by Archimedes of Syracuse at the time of his visit to Egypt. By the use of such screws they carry water in successive lifts as far as the entrance. An enormous amount of water is thrown out, to one's astonishment. By means of a trifling amount of labour the slaves produce for their masters an income beyond belief, but they wear out their own bodies both by day and night in the diggings under the earth. They die in large numbers because of the exceptional hardships. No pause is granted them in their labours. Compelled beneath the blows of their overseers to endure the severity of their plight, they throw their lives away in a wretched manner.
(Diodorus, Greek from Sicily c.100 BC)

■ *What evidence is there that Diodorus sympathised with the slaves?*

■ *What arguments in favour of slavery or forced labour might have been put by other people at the time?*

Hand mills like this were in use not long after Homer's time

Copper and bronze working

Earth or clay

Small air holes to control burning

1 Pile of wood is burned slowly with little oxygen. This makes it into *charcoal* – almost pure carbon.

Blow-pipe with end of baked clay

Mixture of charcoal and crushed ore

Furnace of stone

2 Continuous hard blowing needed to get a temperature of 1000°C.

3 When furnace has cooled the cinders or 'slag' must be broken up to release beads of copper (or tin).

Clay crucible with beads of metal

4 Another furnace. More charcoal. Keep blowing. 1000°C needed.

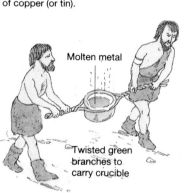

Molten metal

Twisted green branches to carry crucible

5 Take crucible to mould. Keep the green branches wet – and hurry!

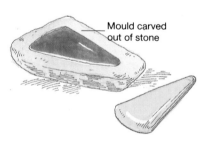

Mould carved out of stone

6 After casting, copper or bronze axes are ready for sharpening.

2 Wood and charcoal

Wood was still the only important fuel, as it had been since fire was discovered. In the city, however, there was a big advantage to be gained by turning it into charcoal before using it. It takes four times as much wood as charcoal to produce the same amount of heat. So the further the fuel had to be carried the more sense it made to use charcoal.

For working metal, charcoal was the only choice. Its use was essential to produce the high temperature needed to smelt copper. Two furnaces and lots of charcoal were needed. Iron is even more difficult to smelt than copper. It needs a much higher temperature of about 2000°C., and this has to be kept up for hours. Iron workers needed bellows to provide a steady blast of air. Iron also had to be heated and hammered over and over again, and this used up enormous amounts of charcoal.

Metal workers had to be highly skilled. There was no way of measuring temperature or time accurately, so that everything depended on the craftsman's eye and his experience. It took him a long time to learn the secrets of his craft. To the ordinary people it seemed that the craftsman shared in the power of the gods.

Source 25 Send 7200 logs of wood

To Sin-idinnen . . . Wood for the metal workers in Dur Gurgurri should be looked into by you. They shall cut for you 7200 logs of wood of a volume of 10, 20 and 40 units, and of a length of 1 unit, 1.5 units and 2 units. Each batch of 200 logs shall be loaded into a freighter and brought to Babylon. Among the fire-wood that shall be cut there shall be no wood that died in the forest. They shall cut green wood only. The fire-wood should be brought quickly lest the metal workers sit down empty-handed. (Letter from King Hammurabi of Babylon (1792–1750BC) to his forest manager.)

■ *Why did the King concern himself with the wood supply?*

It looks as if Hammurabi's metal work was done somewhere near the city of Babylon. Usually as much as possible of the metal working was done wherever the ore and a good supply of wood could be found close together. Such places were often in mountains, perhaps hundreds of kilometres from the city.

- *What advantages would this have?*

- *What problem would it increase?*

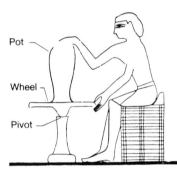

Source 26 A pivot for a potter's wheel from Jericho, about 2000 BC

3 Animal power

Animals for transport

When people had to carry goods by land pack animals were the usual method. We have clear evidence of the use of donkeys from about 3000 BC. A train of pack animals might travel 40 kilometres in a day, but the animals had to be fed and looked after and this made the cost of transport high.

Our first evidence of wheeled carts comes from Mesopotamia, dated about 3500 BC. The ox harness already used to pull ploughs could be applied quite easily to this new purpose.

Pottery made on a wheel has been found in Mesopotamia, dating from about 3500 BC. There is no evidence which came first, the potter's wheel or the cart wheel.

- *Which is more likely to have come first?*

The wheel was a very important invention, but ox-wagons were slow. Fifteen kilometres was a day's journey even on a good road. On soft or rough ground they could hardly move. If goods had to be carried far by land the pack animal remained the main method.

Pot

Wheel

Pivot

Source 27 A potter's wheel, from an Egyptian tomb painting of about 1800 BC

Source 28 *Above*: An Egyptian tomb carving, about 1900 BC. *Below*: A carving in the Royal Palace, Nimrod, Mesopotamia, about 800 BC

Source 29 Ramses II of Egypt (1292–1225 BC). This painting is from his tomb and shows Ramses attacking the Nubians (of southern Sudan)

Source 30 A bronze bit from Egypt, about 1200 BC

Source 31 *Below*: Assurbanipal, King of the Assyrians, 668–633 BC. A carving from his palace at Nineveh, Mesopotamia. Notice that he has not stirrups and uses a cloth instead of a saddle.

■ *Is it likely that he could really shoot arrows while galloping?*

Animals for war

By about 2000 BC horses were being harnessed to chariots. These were light, two-wheeled vehicles which could move at speeds of 30 kph or more. For a thousand years the horse-drawn chariot was a vital weapon. In Egypt, Mesopotamia and China, from 1800 to 800 BC the ruler with the best chariots won the battles.

About 1000 BC the nomadic tribes of Central Asia found out how to ride into battle on the horse itself. Perhaps they had invented better methods of controlling horses.

The chariot went on being used in some backward areas like Britain, but the civilised armies copied the nomads and built up cavalry regiments of their own. The nomads could shoot arrows from horseback, the civilised armies normally used their horses, as they had used their chariots, to move quickly to a point of attack.

Corn

This stone turns

Flour collects here

Source 32 *Left*: Four donkey mills and a baking oven at Pompeii, AD 79 *Far left*: A Roman tomb carving of the second century AD. You can see in what a tight circle the horse turned, in order to drive the mill

Source 33 An ox-powered saqiya. This is a modern picture from Egypt, but machines like this were in use from about 100 BC. As the ox walked round in a circle the wheel of pots in the foreground turned and lifted the water to irrigate the fields

Animals to drive machines

Mills like these, usually powered by donkeys, were common in Roman towns and on large farms. They were in use by about 200 BC. A donkey mill could grind about 15 kilograms of corn an hour, as much as two slaves using hand mills.

At about the same time animal powered mills were developed to crush ore at the copper and silver mines. On the larger Roman farms animal-powered mills crushed olives to produce olive oil.

These early machines were a great step forward. They allowed energy to be used more efficiently, and they meant that animals could do work previously done by people. At the same time machines powered by people were invented, like the Archimedes screw and the Chinese pedal pump.

■ *Why might people in the ancient world have used human beings to drive machines instead of animals?*

Machines like the *noria* on the right were being used in Egypt about 100 BC. It did the same job as the ox-powered version above, but without the ox. The river flowing past the bottom of the wheel turned it and lifted the water. Perhaps it was this that gave some unknown inventor the idea of using water power to turn machines.

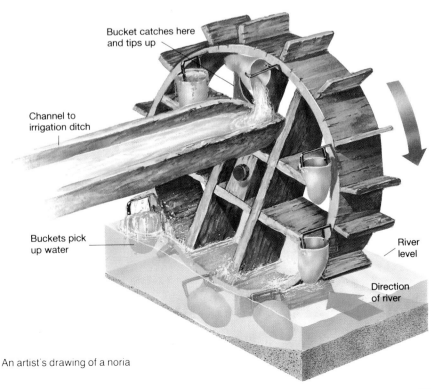

Bucket catches here and tips up

Channel to irrigation ditch

Buckets pick up water

River level

Direction of river

An artist's drawing of a noria

4 A new source of energy: water power

Source 34 This Chinese picture dates from AD 1313, but there is other evidence of mills of this type in China from AD 100

Source 35 This picture of a water wheel from Venafro, Italy, was reconstructed from an impression left in volcanic lava

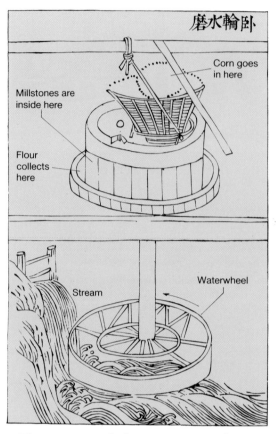

磨水輪卧

Corn goes in here

Millstones are inside here

Flour collects here

Stream

Waterwheel

The source of the energy to drive a machine is known as its prime mover. The prime movers of machines like the Roman corn mills or the Archimedes screw were animals or human beings. In the first century BC we find evidence of a second sort of prime mover – water power. Today we are quite used to machines which turn on their own without any human or animal muscles to push them. To the Greeks it seemed like magic.

Source 36 Water nymphs do the work

Stop your grinding, you women who toil at the mill. Sleep late even though the cocks crow to tell you it is dawn. Demeter, the corn goddess, has ordered the water nymphs to do the work your arms used to do. They leap down on top of the wheel and turn the axle with its revolving spokes. Then it turns the heavy mill-stones.
(Poem by Antipater of Thessalonica, Greece, 1st century BC)

■ *It is not likely that the poet saw water nymphs turn the wheel. Why should he say they did?*

There were two main types of water-wheel, and there is no clear evidence as to which came first.

Mills with horizontal wheels could only be used in fast flowing streams. Mills of this type are known from the hilly areas of Turkey, Greece and Europe as well as from China.

The Roman engineer Vitruvius lived in the last part of the first century BC. He wrote a book in which he described in detail a different type of mill. The first difference was that the Vitruvian mill wheel was placed in a vertical position like the wheel of the *noria*.

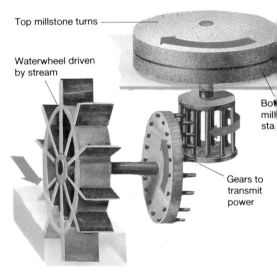

Top millstone turns

Waterwheel driven by stream

Bo mill sta

Gears to transmit power

Mills of the type described by Vitruvius worked like this

The second difference is that the gear-wheels on the Vitruvian mill enabled the millstones to turn five times as fast as the driving wheel.

A mill like the one at Venafro could do as much work as 30 slaves. it could grind 150 kilograms of corn an hour.

Look back at the translation of the poem (Source 36).

■ *Which of the two types of wheel did Antipater have in mind?*

■ *Is it likely that the Chinese type of wheel was copied from the Roman type, or the other way round, or are they likely to have been quite independent inventions?*

Although the Romans knew how to make the Vitruvian type of mill, they did not make many of them. Most of those of which we know were made after AD 200. There is little evidence that the Romans used them to do anything else but grind corn. Nor did this type of mill spread to India or China.

Mills like those on the right were very uncommon in the Roman world. By about AD 400 the corn for the City of Rome itself was probably ground in water-mills, but there were not many anywhere else.

■ *Why not?*

This reconstruction is based on archaeological evidence at Barbegal in southern France. The eight mills could grind 2800 kg of corn an hour, as much as 800 slaves. It was built about AD 310, probably by an engineer called Benignus

■ *What does the existence of these mills suggest about the transport system and the market for corn near Barbegal at the time?*

Wind and water for transport

Water power, and with it wind power, had been used for transport long before the first water-mills were made.

It is no accident that the early civilisations were in river valleys or on coastlands. The steady flow of a river provided free energy to carry goods by raft or boat. The wind was another source of free energy that could be harnessed as soon as sails had been developed. Many hunter-gatherers had

been skilled canoe makers and fishermen, but it was the early city dwellers who made the first ships.

None of the sailors of ancient times could find their way at sea when far out of sight of land, and their ships could not sail except when the wind was behind them. But they could and did carry goods regularly for hundreds of kilometres. Early civilisations would have been much poorer without them.

Source 37 This Egyptian painting of a sailing ship dates from about 3100 BC. It is probably the earliest picture of a sail in use

Source 38 Egyptian ships, from a temple carving, about 1480 BC

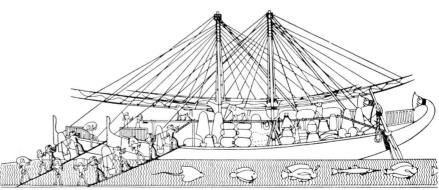

Changes and developments 3500 BC–AD 500

By AD 500 there were *probably* about 190 million people in the world. Most lived in Asia, North Africa and Europe, where farming was well established. They were able to use the energy of animals for transport and for war as well as for work on the farm. But the human energy of slaves and peasants still did most of the hard work. Wind power was in use for sailing ships, and trade had begun to link up some civilised areas.

Machines powered by animals had been known for nearly a thousand years. A second prime mover, the water-mill, was slowly coming into use.

The only fuel of importance was still wood, but it was now sometimes used in the form of charcoal. Skilled craftsmen used it to make metal goods of all kinds, from beautiful ornaments to the weapons of war.

Most of the energy developments of this period had begun in Mesopotamia or Egypt. But by AD 500 China was moving into the lead.

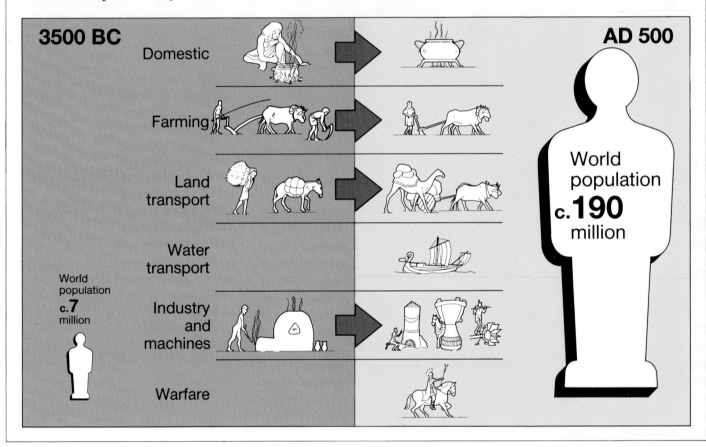

The Middle Ages 500–1500

The collapse of Roman power during the fifth century AD led to chaos and disorder in Western Europe. Trade almost stopped. People fled from the towns. In some areas, like Britain, it looked as if civilisation was destroyed.

This does not mean that technical skills like iron-working, pottery or farming were lost. Even in Roman times most people were country folk who grew their own food, and their lives went on much as before. There is so little evidence about life in Western Europe from about AD 500 to 800 that we call this the 'Dark Ages'. But when this gap in the evidence ends people had better ploughs than the Romans used, and oxen to pull them. They had good axes and other iron tools. Most important, they had water mills to grind corn.

Many people were killed during the disorders of the 'Dark Ages', but the skills that survived and the plentiful energy supplies of its forests and rivers would eventually make Europe strong and rich. But for a long time after the fall of Rome, Western Europe was a rather backward part of the world. The leading civilisation was that of China.

Source 39 An Anglo-Saxon plough, from a tenth-century manuscript

Developments in China and the Middle East

The name 'Middle Ages' does not make much sense in Chinese history.

Civilisation continued there without any real break from about 200 BC to the present day. During the years from AD 200 to AD 1300 the Chinese made many important new technical developments. For example, Chinese iron working was better than that of the Romans. The Chinese were able to get the furnace much hotter, so that the iron became liquid. It could then be poured into moulds of any shape as 'cast iron'. One reason why the Chinese could do this was because they had better bellows to provide a continuous blast of air. Another Chinese invention was the horse collar. Before this period a horse pulling a load pulled against a strap which went round its throat and tended to choke it. The Chinese padded collar spread the load on to the horse's shoulders. This enabled a horse to pull four times as heavy a load as with the old throat strap. The Chinese also improved the horse saddle and may have invented stirrups.

Egyptian and Roman ships had only been able to sail reliably with the wind behind them. They had to keep close to land so as to know where they were. The Chinese made three improvements. They improved sails so that ships could sail into the wind. They invented the compass with which they could navigate out of sight of land. And they developed the rudder with which they could steer more accurately.

Perhaps the most famous Chinese invention was gunpowder – a new form of energy which could be used in war.

During the European 'Dark Ages' there also grew up a powerful and brilliant Islamic civilisation in the Middle East and North Africa. It was in this region that a new prime mover, the windmill, was invented.

Developments spread from East to West

- *Ideas like these may have started in other places about which we have less evidence than we have about China. Where else might the idea of the horse collar or stirrups have started?*

- *Which inventions may well have been made independently in Western Europe?*

- *Why might some inventions have spread more quickly than others?*

- *Why should the Iranians make windmills, instead of using watermills?*

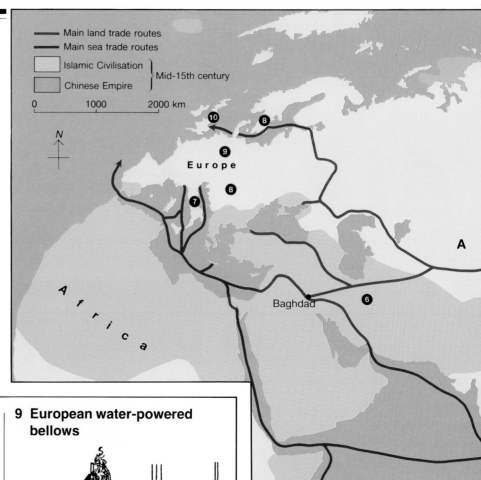

Legend:
— Main land trade routes
— Main sea trade routes
□ Islamic Civilisation
□ Chinese Empire } Mid-15th century

0   1000   2000 km

N

Europe

Africa

Baghdad

A

Europe

7 The European windmill

Source 46 European windmills looked like this. They had sails which turned vertically, like European water-wheels. The earliest evidence is from AD 1180. From an Italian fourteenth century manuscript

8 European stirrups

Source 47 Iron stirrups from Hungary (sixth century) and Sweden (eighth century)

9 European water-powered bellows

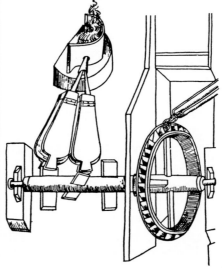

Source 48 Bellows at a European iron works. From a fifteenth century German manuscript

10 Gunpowder in Europe

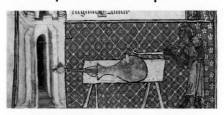

Source 49 The earliest European picture of a gun, from England, 1326

6 Windmills

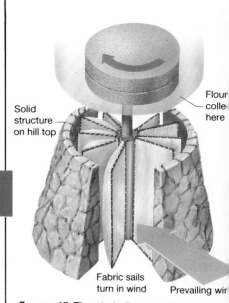

Solid structure on hill top

Flour colle here

Fabric sails turn in wind

Prevailing wir

Source 45 The windmill, a new prime mover. The earliest windmills had sails which turned horizontally like Chinese water-wheels. Mills like this were first built in Iran in AD 900. From an Arab drawing, about 1300

Energy inventions in the middle ages

Invention	First evidence in the East	in Western Europe	Some clues to the spread of ideas
Cast iron	200BC (China)	AD1350	Only possible with powerful bellows.
Water-powered bellows	AD200 (China)	AD1350	The European bellows were quite different (Source 56, page 33).
Coal used in smelting iron	AD400 China	AD1709	Europeans used coke in a quite different process.
Horse collar	AD475 (China)	cAD1000	
Fore-and-aft sails	AD200 (China)	AD1400	These sails were used by Arabs from about AD700.
Rudder	AD200 China	AD1180	
Compass	AD1090 (China)	AD1269	
Stirrups	AD477 (China)	cAD750	Known in Hungary AD560 and used by Vikings in N.W. Europe c 750.
Windmill	AD900 (Iran)	AD1180	European windmills were different in design.
Gunpowder	cAD1000 (China)	cAD1300	

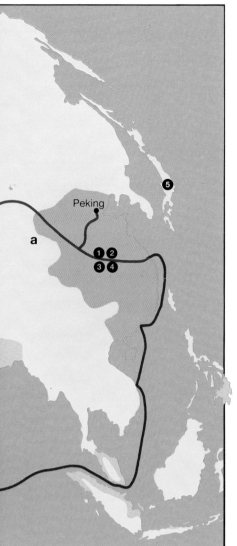

The Far East

1 Iron working

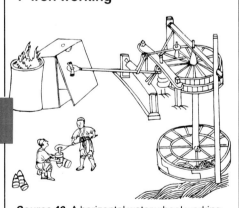

Source 40 A horizontal water wheel working the bellows for a blast furnace. The iron was made in clay crucibles which can be seen in the foreground. This had another advantage: coal could be used instead of charcoal, without harming the iron. From a Chinese book, Nung Shu, AD 1313

2 Rudder, compass and improved sails

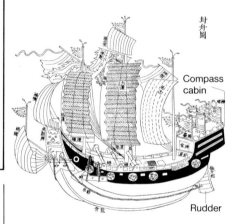

封舟圖

Compass cabin

Rudder

Source 41 This picture is from a Chinese book, printed in AD 1757, but the type of ship had not changed since the Middle Ages

3 Padded horse collar

Source 42 Copy of a painting made in AD 951, showing the padded horse collar

4 Stirrups and the saddle

Source 43 A model horse found in a Chinese tomb, AD 701. The stirrups and the improved saddle enabled soldiers to fight on horseback

5 Gunpowder

Source 44 A grenade bursting near a Japanese bowman. From a drawing of 1292

31

Europe begins to catch up 1000–1500

After about AD 1000 the Western Europeans began to catch up rapidly.

The time of disorder that had followed the collapse of the Roman Empire was over. The Europeans began to build great cathedrals and castles. They had scholars, artists, craftsmen and traders. They were also able to learn from other more advanced civilisations.

■ *What energy uses did the Europeans inherit from the Romans?*

■ *What ideas about energy use may they have learned from the Chinese or from Islam?*

Europe had many natural energy resources. There was an ample supply of water power and plenty of wood for fuel. There was also fertile land to grow grass and oats to feed oxen and horses. Once the Europeans were able to make full use of the available resources, they could become rich and powerful.

Watermills and windmills in Europe

The Roman design of watermill had never been forgotten. In countries like France and England, where there were many fast flowing rivers, mills were built in large numbers. The Domesday Book gives information about 3000 villages in England. Between them they had 5624 watermills; one for every 50 people.

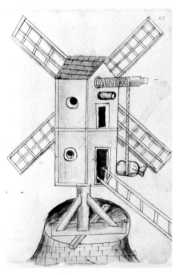

Source 50 *Above*: Wind power used to hoist the sacks of corn. From a fifteenth century German manuscript

Source 51 A Mill in 1086
Manor of Halesowen, Worcestershire. Earl Roger holds Salwarpe . . . On the demesne (the Earl's land) is one plough, and six villeins (peasants) and 5 bordars (poor peasants) have seven ploughs. There are three serfs and three bondwomen and a mill worth 10 shillings (50p) and five saltpans worth 60 shillings (£3).
(*Domesday Book*, Compiled for William the Conqueror, 1086 England)

The earliest written mention of a windmill in Europe comes from about 1180. Some historians think that the Crusaders brought the idea back from the Middle East. The first Crusade was in 1097 and the second in 1147.

■ *Do the dates fit?*

Source 52 This is the earliest European drawing of a windmill. It is from the illuminated initial of a psalm book made at Canterbury about 1270

Source 53 This diagram of a water-powered corn mill was drawn by the abbess of a twelfth century abbey. Corn is being poured in by one of the nuns while on the right an angel lends a hand

■ *Why should the abbess make a drawing like this?*

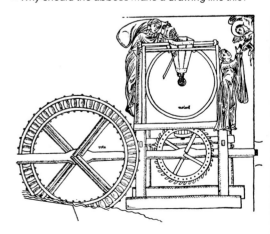

Other historians point out that the eastern windmills were horizontal ones like the picture on page 30. They think that the European mill with its vertical sails and its gearing is more likely to be based on the European watermill.

■ *Which opinion is more likely? Could both views be true?*

Mills cost a lot of money to build. In 1342, for instance, the Abbot of Glastonbury spent £11.12s.11d (£11.65) building a new corn mill in the village of Walton. It was a very large investment of money. The reason why it was worth making was that the Abbot was Lord of the Manor. This gave him the right to compel the villagers to have their corn ground at his mill. Of course he didn't run the mill himself. He rented it out to a miller, usually one of the richer village people. William Pyntel was the Miller at Walton, and he paid a rent of £3 a year to the Abbot.

■ *Did the Abbot make a good bargain?*

Source 54 Abbot Samson of Bury St Edmunds loses his temper

Herbert the Dean set up a windmill at Habardun. When the Abbot heard this he grew so hot with anger than he would scarcely eat or speak a single word. On the morrow he ordered the Sacrist to send carpenters to pull everything down. Hearing this, the Dean came and said that he had a right to do this. Free benefit of the wind should not be denied to any man. He said also that he wished to grind his own corn there and not the corn of others.

To this the Abbot, still angry, made answer, 'I thank you as I should thank you if you had cut off both my feet. By God's face I will never eat bread till that building be thrown down. Go away, he said. Before you reach your house you shall hear what will be done with your mill.'

But the Dean, shrinking with fear from the face of the Abbot caused the mill to be pulled down by his own servants without delay.

(Chronicle of Jocelyn of Brakelond, AD 1191)

■ *Why was the Abbot so determined to pull down the windmill?*

By the end of the Middle Ages there were watermills and windmills all over Europe. A new craftsman, the millwright, was needed to make and mend these mills. As well as being clever with his hands he had to be mechanically minded – to know about gear wheels and machinery. He was just the sort of person to invent new machinery if it was needed. By the end of the Middle Ages there were hundreds of millwrights in every country in Europe.

New uses for mills

The people of Europe in the Middle Ages used the power of wind and water mills for many other things as well as grinding corn. There were saw mills, mills to grind and sharpen tools, mills to make paper, mills to pump water, and mills for many other purposes.

The Chinese idea of using water power to work hammers and bellows in the iron industry was in use in Europe by about 1300. This change was very important. Much more iron could now be made in Europe – enough to make many more horse-shoes, iron tools, or guns.

Source 55 *Above*: This mill is being used to treat woollen cloth. The picture was drawn in 1617, but mills of this sort were in use in the thirteenth century

Source 56 One water wheel works a blast furnace. Three others work trip hammers. From a German book, about 1565

33

Horses become widely used in Europe

Peaceful use of horses

The horse-collar was quite common in Europe by 1200.

Using it a horse could pull as much as the ox but twice as fast (about 5 kilometres an hour). This meant that it could do twice as much work as an ox. The extra speed was of great importance for transport. Transport of goods over land by heavy wagon became cheaper.

The improved harness also made the horse more useful on the farm.

Source 58 *Left*: From the Luttrell Psalter, England, about 1338. *Above*: From a Flemish book illustration, 1473. These pictures show the arrangement of ropes and wooden bars which enabled horses to pull a plough – or anything else that needed pulling. Horses harnessed like this were to be the most convenient moveable source of energy until the coming of the tractor in the twentieth century

War-horses

The knights who were skilled at fighting on horseback, and the barons who led them became the most important class of people in Europe. Heavy horses had to be specially bred to carry the knights, and a much improved type of horseshoe was needed as well. When King Richard I of England went on crusade in 1189 he ordered 50000 horseshoes from the iron-workers in the Forest of Dean in Gloucestershire.

The Europeans had an ample supply of horses and of iron for armour and weapons. This enabled them to hold their own against more civilised people like the Arabs, and sometimes to beat them. The Europeans were taking full advantage of their plentiful sources of energy.

Source 57 Knights in battle. Stirrups and a plentiful supply of iron made this method of fighting possible. From a fifteenth century manuscript

Changes and developments 500–1500

In 1500 AD most people in the world still used wood for fuel and muscle power for work, in a way not very different from the people of Rome or even of earlier times. Most people were still peasants growing their own food.

Great improvements had been made in harnessing animals and in using water and wind power. Better transport had helped some of these ideas to spread.

But probably the largest city in the world was Mexico City where about 100000 people lived with a technology much simpler than that of ancient Egypt. The Mexicans had no draught animals, no wheeled vehicles, no water mills and no iron.

The most populous country in the world was China, with about 100 million people, nearly a quarter of the world's total. China had a very highly developed energy technology.

During the Middle Ages Western Europeans started to catch up. They inherited some energy techniques from Rome. They learned some others from the more advanced civilisations of China and Islam. They developed some for themselves.

Nature provided Western Europe with abundant energy resources – water power, wind power, wood and food for horses and oxen. By 1500 the Europeans had been making good use of water power wind power, and horse power for some centuries. They had a ship with which they could use the free energy of the trade winds and ocean currents to sail and carry goods to almost any part of the world. Their guns were more powerful than the weapons available to any other people.

Until about 1500 Europeans had not played a very important part in world history. They were now in a position to take the lead.

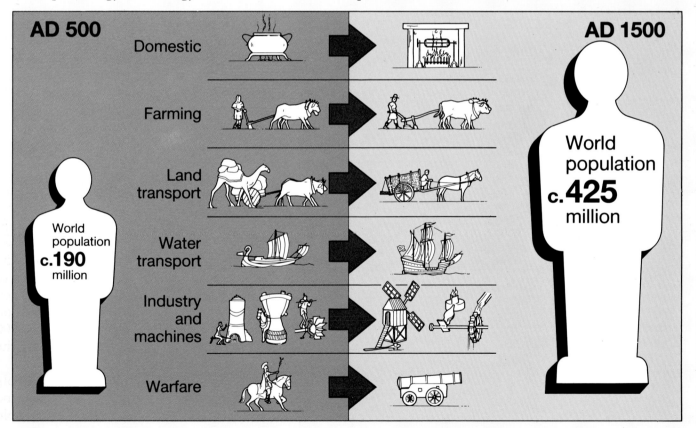

AD 500 — AD 1500

Domestic
Farming
Land transport
Water transport
Industry and machines
Warfare

World population c.190 million

World population c.425 million

4

The second energy revolution 1500–1875

The first 'energy revolution' was based mainly on wood, animal power and water power. Between AD 1500 and 1800 the people of Europe made such full use of these long-established resources that they brought about a second energy revolution. This was based mainly on coal and steam.

■ *Why did it happen?*

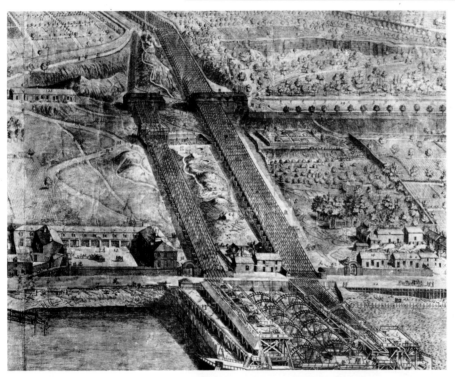

Source 59 King Louis XIV of France had this machine built in 1682 to pump water to the fountains in his garden at the Palace of Versailles. It developed 75 horse power

The high water mark of low energy civilisation

The years 1500–1800 were a time of great prosperity and power for Western Europe. The population rose; in France it went up from about 12 million to nearly 30 million. Cities grew even faster: London went up from 120 000 to 900 000.

There were many reasons for this prosperity – rich farmlands, skilled craftsmen, enterprising merchants. But good supplies of energy were an important factor.

Most water wheels were smaller than

Source 60 A view of the Tower of London from the east, 1805, by William Daniell

Sailing ships

Windmills

Watermills

Coal

Horses

Oxen

Wood

European energy resources, about 1800. A modern French historian has estimated that there were 24 million oxen, 14 million horses and 2 million water mills in Europe, as well as windmills and sailing ships for which no reliable figures existed. 200 million tonnes of wood and 12 million tonnes of coal were used per year

the one at Versailles, but there were thousands of them in every country in Europe. There were also many other sources of energy.

The Europeans burned about 200 million tonnes of wood, and over 12 million tonnes of coal as well as using the energy of animals, wind and water. It is impossible to be sure how much useful energy they got from the wood and coal. But if the energy from the other sources is added up and divided by the total population, each European had at least three 'energy slaves' in 1800, and several more if the energy from the fuel could be counted. The Europeans were making the most of their excellent natural resources.

What is thy will, Oh Master?

Each European had at least three 'energy' slaves in 1800

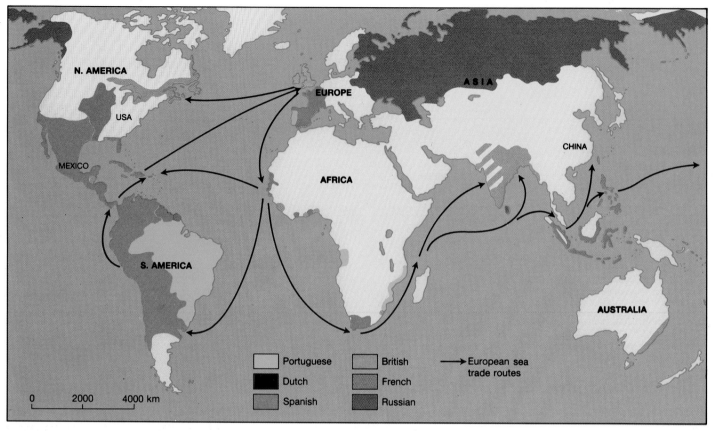

European empires, about 1800

Europe and the World 1500–1800

In the years 1500–1800 Europeans used ships like the one below to conquer America. Africa and part of Asia.

In 1519 Hernando Cortes led 608 Spaniards and 16 horses in an attack on the Aztec Empire of Mexico. There were about 5 million Mexicans, but in two years he had overcome them. One reason why Cortes won was because the Mexicans were divided amongst themselves. What other reasons do the following sources suggest?

Source 61 The 'Sovereign of the Seas', from a contemporary print. This English warship was built in 1637. She was of 1522 tons and had 100 guns. These fired iron balls weighing 9, 12 or 16 kilos. A ship like this could carry several hundred armed men, and could go almost anywhere in the world. Nothing could stand against it – except another European ship

Source 62 Cortes' first battle with the Mexicans

The enemy were so numerous that they covered the whole savannah. They rushed on us like mad dogs, completely surounding us. More than 70 of our men were wounded in the first attack. But with our muskets and crossbows and good sword-play we put up a stout fight. Our artilleryman Mesa killed many of them with his cannon. But we could not drive them off. There were 300 indians to every one of us.

Just at that moment we caught sight of our horsemen. The indians did not at once see them. The plain was bare and the horsemen came quickly upon them and speared them as they chose. As soon as we saw the horsemen we attacked the enemy so vigorously that, caught between the horsemen and ourselves they soon turned tail. The indians thought at that time that horse and rider were one creature, for they had never seen a horse before.
(Bernal Diaz: *The Conquest of New Spain*, Mexico, 1574)

Coal, iron and steam

Wood shortage and the shift to coal

The growing power and wealth of Europeans helped them to conquer other lands. This power was based partly on heavy use of energy supplies, especially wood for the iron industry. In some parts of Europe a serious shortage of wood began about the year 1600.

Source 63 Not enough wood

Within a man's memory it was held impossible to have any want (shortage) of wood in England. But (there) hath been great expense cf timber for navigation, with the infinite increase of building houses, with great expense of wood to make household furniture, caskes and other vessels not to be numbered, and cartes and coaches, besides the extreame waste of wood in making of iron, burning of brick and tile . . . At the present, through the great consuming of wood as aforesaid and the neglect of planting woods, there is a great scarcity of wood throughout the whole kingdom, not only in the City of London and all haven towns but in very many parts within land.
(Stow: *Annals*, London 1605)

Source 64 Shortage makes prices rise

The price of the necessities of life will constantly increase, and the growing scarcity of firewood will be the cause.
(Sully, French Finance Minister, 1610)

Source 65 Poor people burn cow dung

Peterborough . . . as I passed the road I saw upon the walls of ordinary people's houses and their outhouses, the cow dung plastered up to drie in cakes which they use for firing. It's very offensive fewell but the country people use little else in these parts.
(Celia Fiennes: *Journeys*, 1697)

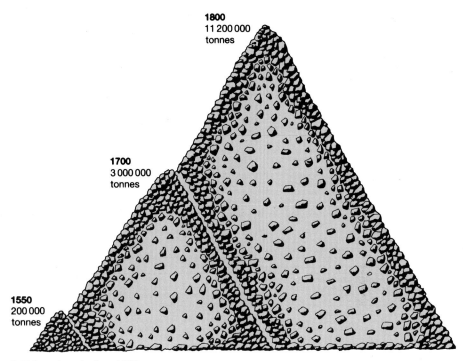

British coal production, 1550–1800

1800 11 200 000 tonnes

1700 3 000 000 tonnes

1550 200 000 tonnes

Source 66 Little timber left

Scarcely any timber remains except at long distances inland. The carriage of it will cost too much for us to be able to make use of it. Wood for building on land and for building ships as well as heating is extremely scarce and dear. It will be more so in the future.
(Report of Deputy (MP) in Brittany, France, 1701)

- *In which areas was the shortage most serious according to these sources?*
- *Which areas of Europe would still have plenty of wood?*
- *What evidence is there that the shortage was partly a transport problem?*

Coal had been used in some places for a long time. The Romans and the Chinese had used it. But coal gives off unpleasant fumes and smoke, and is heavy to carry, so in earlier periods it was never very important.

Source 67 The different stages of charcoal burning. Wood was placed around a pole to a height of about 2.5 metres. This was covered with straw, fern and turf. The pole was then removed and burning charcoal dropped down into the stack which then burnt for five or six days

The main British coalfield was on Tyneside. The mines there had been used on a small scale since the twelfth century. Many of them were not far from the river Tyne. From there ships could carry the coal to London – or anywhere else on the coast of Britain or Europe. No other coal mines in Europe were so conveniently placed. So as the price of wood went up, the miners of Tyneside produced more and more coal. By 1700 British output was five times as much as *the rest of the world* put together. About a million tonnes a year were sold to other European countries.

Source 68 News from Newcastle

England's a perfect World! Has Indies too!
Correct your maps; Newcastle is Peru!
Let naughty Spaniards triumph 'til
   they're told
Our sooty mineral purifies their gold.
(From an anonymous pamphlet, 1651.
The main mines in the Spanish Empire
(the Indies) were in Peru.)

In the seventeenth century the British still used a great deal of wood as fuel. But London and many other parts of the country could not have managed without coal.

Source 69 Forced to use coal

The inhabitants in general are forced to make their fires of sea-coale or pit-coale, even in the chambers of honourable personages . . . Through necessity which is the mother of all arts, they have of very late years discovered the making of tin, the making of glass and the burning of brick with sea coale or pit coale.
(Stow: *Annals*, 1605)

As well as the industries that Stow mentions, there were others which needed fuel. Sugar was being imported from America and had to be refined. Other industries like soap making and brewing beer were now being done on a large scale in the towns. Britain's growing prosperity depended on her good supplies of coal.

Coal causes problems

Pollution in the home and street

Source 70 Ladies dislike the smell
Within 30 years last, the nice dames of London would not come into any house or room where sea coles were burned, nor willingly eat of the meat that was either boiled or roasted with a sea cole fire . . .
(Stow: *Annals*, London 1605)

Source 71 A London fog
London, by reason of the excessive coldness of the air hindering the ascent of the smoke, was so filled with the sooty steam of the sea-coal, that one could hardly see across the streets. Filling the lungs with the gross particles (of soot) exceedingly obstructed the breast, so that one could scarcely breathe.
(Diary of John Evelyn, 24 January 1684)

The new grates and chimneys cut down the pollution inside the houses of the people who could afford them. Outside in the street the problem got steadily worse.

Problems in industry
Part of the problem of air pollution from coal burning is due to sulphur fumes in the smoke. In most industries this did little harm to the product, however much the neighbours complained. But two industries had real difficulties. They were brewing and iron working.

The fumes from coal fires spoiled the malt used to make beer. So the brewers had to use wood, even though it cost much more.

Source 72 London brewers complain
Wood cannot be gott to serve all our needs without great ruin and decay to the whole city.
(Petition of London brewers to Sir F. Walsingham, Secretary of State, 1578).

The problem in the iron industry was much more serious. The sulphur in coal ruined every attempt to use it in blast furnaces. By 1700 British iron produc-

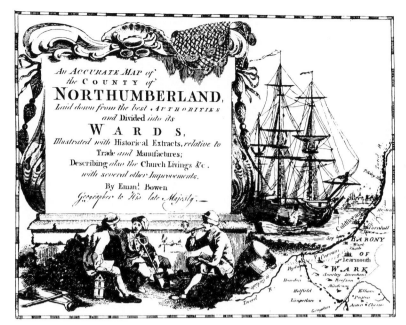

Source 73 Miners and seamen, with a collier in the background. From a map, about 1760

tion was declining. English iron-masters moved to remote places where wood for charcoal was still available. More and more they bought their iron from Sweden where there was no shortage of trees.

Problems in the mines
As more coal was used and the miners had to dig deeper they ran more and more into the problem of flooding. By 1700 this was very serious in the British coal mines. Some of them were over 100 metres deep.

Source 74 An eighteenth century coal-burning grate. A coal fire needs an iron grate and a specially built chimney to provide a good draught. Otherwise it smokes and gives off fumes of sulphur. During the seventeenth century many houses were rebuilt with chimneys and grates designed for coal. Drawing based on museum materials

The problems of using coal are solved

The brewers find an answer

About 1640 the brewers of Derby found how to use coal without spoiling the beer.

Heaps of coal were carefully covered with clay, and then allowed to burn very slowly. When the fire was extinguished, the coal had turned into coke, which did no harm to the beer.

The solution in the iron-works

As the diagram shows there were three stages at which a lot of fuel had to be used. Coal was suitable for the last of these, but charcoal was essential for the other two. As long as this was true for either of them it would be cheaper to import ready-made Swedish bar iron.

The problem was solved in three steps.

1 1709. Abraham Darby of Coalbrookdale, Shropshire, found a way of using coke in the blast furnace. He could make good cast-iron objects like cooking pots and, later on, cylinders for steam engines. But the pig iron he made was not suitable for refining into wrought iron. Darby had half-solved the problem of using coal in the first stage of iron working.

2 1740–80. Much better blowing engines were developed, using steam power. This meant that the blast furnace could be bigger and hotter. With this very hot furnace, even using coke as fuel, the pig iron was suitable for refining at the forge. The problem of using coal for stage 1 was now fully solved.

Source 75 Above: Charring coal to make coke. From a French book, 1773

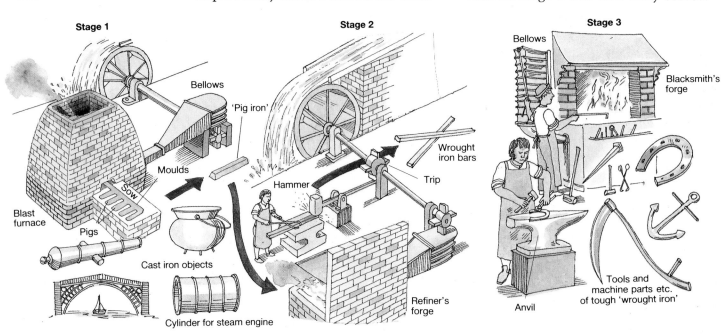

Stage 1

Bellows

'Pig iron'

Moulds

Sow

Blast furnace

Pigs

Cast iron objects

Cylinder for steam engine

Stage 2

Wrought iron bars

Trip

Hammer

Refiner's forge

Stage 3

Bellows

Blacksmith's forge

Tools and machine parts etc. of tough 'wrought iron'

Anvil

The main stages in the production of iron in Britain in the eighteenth century

Source 76 A drawing of Coalbrookdale by C. Vivares, 1758

■ What is being made on the right of the picture just beyond the fence?
■ What is being carried on the cart moving across the picture?

Source 78 A German doctor, George Agricola, published an illustrated book on mining in 1556.

Far left: This drawing shows three pumps worked by a single water wheel on the surface
Left: Other machines for pumping or for lifting loads from the mine were powered by horses

3 1783–4. Henry Cort made a new type of furnace, the 'Pudding Furnace', to refine the pig iron, and a rolling mill which used steam power to shape the wrought iron. The pudding furnace used raw coal. Cort's process worked with pig iron made in a coke-fired blast furnace. Charcoal iron was still thought to be better, but Cort's process was fifteen times as fast and so the iron was far cheaper. Cort had solved the problem of using coal in stage 2.

The problem was now solved. With plenty of cheap coal available there seemed to be no limit to the amount of iron that could be made. Iron rail-roads and iron ships became possible, as well as iron machines of all sorts.

- *Could the change from using wood as fuel in iron works to using coal have happened any earlier?*

- *What other invention had to be made first?*

The solution in the mines

The British coal mines were deep enough to run into very serious pumping problems in the seventeenth century. The German silver and copper miners had already been troubled by flooding and German mining engineers had invented ingenious systems of pumps. These machines were copied by British miners. But by 1700 they could barely keep pace with the flood-water, as the mines went deeper and deeper.

Source 77 Pumps had to work on Sunday

I went a mile farther on and came to where they were digging in the mines. There was at least twenty mines in sight, which employs a great many people at work almost day and night, but constantly all and every day including the Lord's Day, which they are forced to do to prevent their mines being overflowed with water. They have great expense to drain the mines with mills that horses turn, and now they have the mills or engines that are turned by water . . . They are the sort that turn the water into many towns that I have seen about London, Darby, Exeter and many places more. They do five times more good than the mills they used to use, but they are more costly. (Celia Fiennes. Celia wrote her diary of her travels in 1697. In this passage she is describing the Cornish tin mines. She might have said as much about coalmines.)

- *How can you tell from this source that the problem was desperate?*

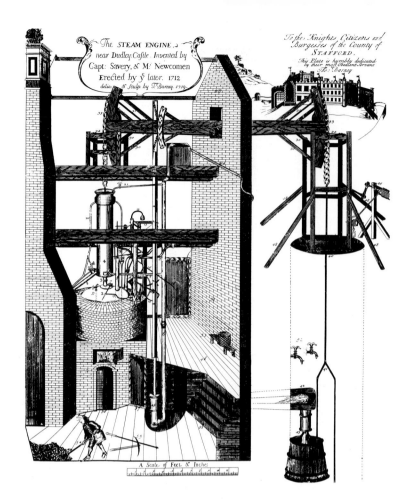

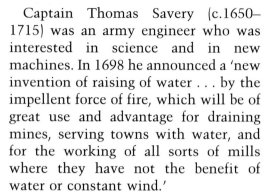

Source 79 The first Newcomen engine, erected at Dudley, 1712. A contemporary drawing

The power of steam

Source 80 A new force

The difficulties that miners and colliers labour under by the frequent disorders and cumbersomeness of water engines, encouraged me to invent new engines to work by the new force.
(Savery: *The Miner's Friend* 1707)

Captain Thomas Savery (c.1650–1715) was an army engineer who was interested in science and in new machines. In 1698 he announced a 'new invention of raising of water . . . by the impellent force of fire, which will be of great use and advantage for draining mines, serving towns with water, and for the working of all sorts of mills where they have not the benefit of water or constant wind.'

Savery's machine was completed in 1702. It worked, but it often broke, and was never used in the mines.

It was Thomas Newcomen who invented the first succesful steam engine in 1712. He was a Cornish blacksmith and ironmonger. He sold tools and iron to the tin miners, so he knew about their pumping problems and the sort of pumps they used. In his machine he used one of the familiar pumps to lift the water. The diagram shows the clever way in which he used steam to work it.

Newcomen's engine could be made by a skilled craftsman like Newcomen himself. It needed no specially strong metals, because it worked by atmospheric presure. This is probably why it succeeded.

Newcomen's 'fire engine' solved the problem of pumping water from the coal mines. By 1750 most large coal mines in Britain had a Newcomen engine, and several had been built in other countries.

How the Newcomen engine worked

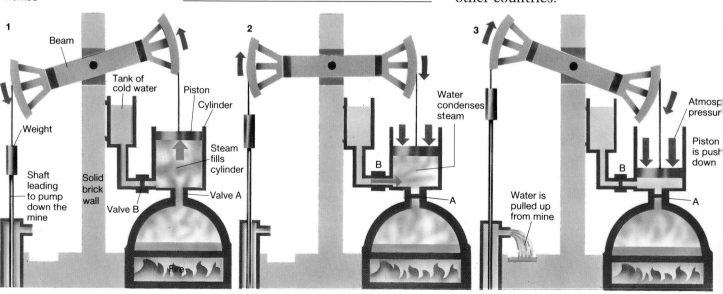

Accurate craftsmanship
The cylinder of Watt's engine had to be kept above 100° C and the condenser had to be kept as cold as possible. No steam had to leak past the piston. So all the working parts had to be made much more accurately than was usual with large machines.

Governor

Link motion

Other smaller inventions
Watt and a team of skilled craftsmen had to design and make parts like the governor, the link motion, and the valve gear.

Flywheel: other machines can be driven from this wheel

This pipe brings steam from the boiler

High quality castings
The cylinder had to be accurately cast and then bored out to precise dimensions. If this was wrong steam would leak and the engine would not work.

Valve gear

Capital
All these things cost a great deal of money. At one time Boulton and Watt had to borrow £17 000 from the banks. They began to work together in 1773, but it was 1784 before they were out of debt.

Separate condenser

Source 81 A Watt rotative engine in the Science Museum, London

The steam engine takes over

Several engineers made improvements to the Newcomen engine. The most important was James Watt.

Watt was trained as a scientific instrument maker, not as an engineer. He worked at Glasgow University, and was a friend of Joseph Black, the Professor of Chemistry. At the time, Black was working out new ways of measuring the heat used to turn water into steam, and Watt made the instruments he used. Watt was asked to mend the University's model of a steam pump. When he measured the heat it used, he found that it was mostly wasted. How could this be prevented? Watt puzzled over this for two years. Then, in 1765, he suddenly saw that if the steam was condensed into water in a separate chamber instead of in the cylinder, much of the loss could be saved. He called his invention the 'separate condenser'. It meant that his engine used less than half as much coal as a Newcomen engine doing the same work.

This was only the first of a long series of Watt's inventions. The most impor-tant of these led to the rotative engine.

The first engine of this type was made by Watt and his partner Matthew Boulton in 1782. It was a great step forward because it could turn a wheel steadily and reliably. This meant that it could be used to drive different sorts of machine. Until 1782 the steam engine had just been a pump. Now it was a new prime mover – the first since the windmill.

Table 1 First practical use of steam power for various purposes

Year	Use	
1712	Pump water	Thomas Newcomen, Warwickshire
1776	Blowing engine in Shropshire iron works	John Wilkinson, Shropshire
1782	Hammer in forge	John Wilkinson, Shropshire
1784	Mine winding engine	Cornwall
1785	Cotton spinning mill	Papplewick, Lancashire
1785	Brewery	Whitbread, London
1786	Flour Mill	Albion Mill, London
1807	Boat	Robert Fulton, U.S.A.
1807	Mine ventilation system	J. Buddle, Hebburn, Tyneside
1814	Railway locomotive	G. Stephenson, Tyneside

■ *Five of these 'firsts' come within the same 5 year period. Why?*

Steam power: the last link in the chain

The stories of coal, iron and steam are linked together. Each played a part in that of the other. This makes it difficult to disentangle the causes of these important developments.

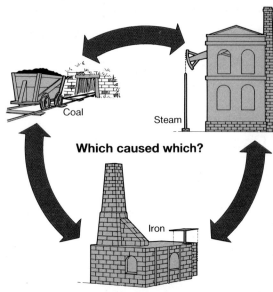

Which caused which?

- *Coal, iron and steam all developed together in Britain. How far could any of them have gone without the other two?*

- *What other factors helped to encourage the development of all three?*

Steam, coal and iron in England and Wales, about 1800

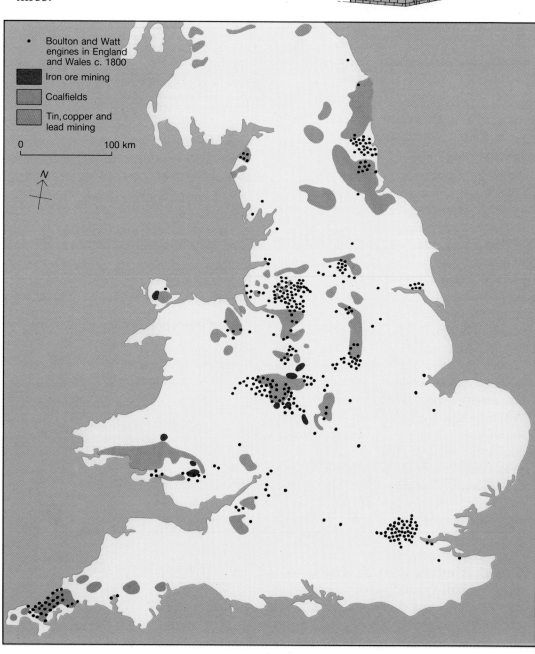

- Boulton and Watt engines in England and Wales c. 1800

Iron ore mining

Coalfields

Tin, copper and lead mining

0   100 km

The energy revolution and the industrial revolution

Change and revolution

The changes in coal mining and in steam power which took place in Britain during the eighteenth century mark a very important stage in the history of energy. Three important turning points came at about the same time.

1 There was a vast increase in coal production. For the next 200 years it seemed as if the world had tapped an unlimited source of energy.

2 The steam engine was the first machine that could turn one sort of energy, the heat of the furnace, into another, mechanical power to lift water or turn wheels. It was the first 'heat engine'. Without it, and other later heat engines like those in cars, the modern 'high energy' way of life would be impossible.

3 Up to this time most of the energy used by men and women had been 'renewable'. It came from wood, from animals, from water or the wind, all sources that are replaced naturally. But coal is a fossil, made in the geological past and never likely to be renewed. The same is true of oil and natural gas. Since 1700 the high energy countries have been using up resources which can never be replaced.

These three changes, taken together, amount to an energy revolution.

The turning points in energy use were closely linked with another great change in industry and society, the industrial revolution. The industrial revolution was partly the cause and partly the result of the energy revolution.

In the year 1700 three out of every four people in Britain lived by farming. By 1875 only about one in ten did so. Between these dates Britain became the first country in the world in which most people live in towns and most goods are produced in factories.

This change may be as important in human history as that from hunting to farming, which began 10000 years ago in the Middle East. Like that earlier change it is certainly of great importance in the history of energy.

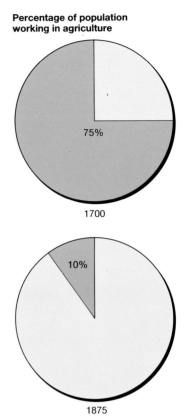

Percentage of population working in agriculture

75%

1700

10%

1875

Percentage of British people working in agriculture, 1700 and 1875

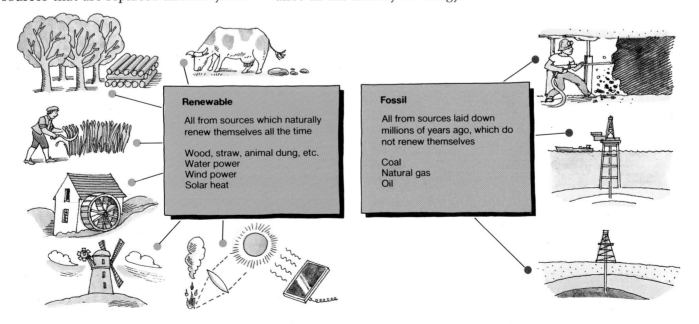

Renewable

All from sources which naturally renew themselves all the time

Wood, straw, animal dung, etc.
Water power
Wind power
Solar heat

Fossil

All from sources laid down millions of years ago, which do not renew themselves

Coal
Natural gas
Oil

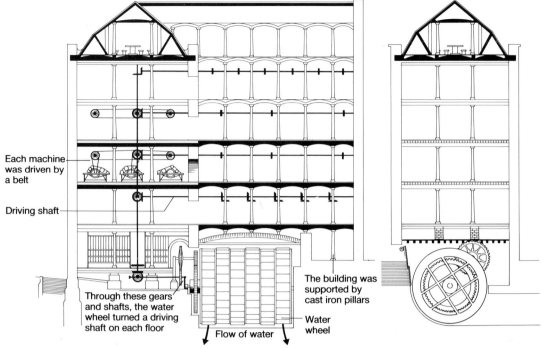

Source 82 North Mill, Belper; built in 1804 by William Strutt. It cost Strutt about £7000. (A skilled cotton spinner at the time might earn 26 shillings = £1.30p a week From an encyclopaedia, 1819

Each machine was driven by a belt

Driving shaft

Through these gears and shafts, the water wheel turned a driving shaft on each floor

Flow of water

The building was supported by cast iron pillars

Water wheel

Cotton imports into Britain, 1760–1875

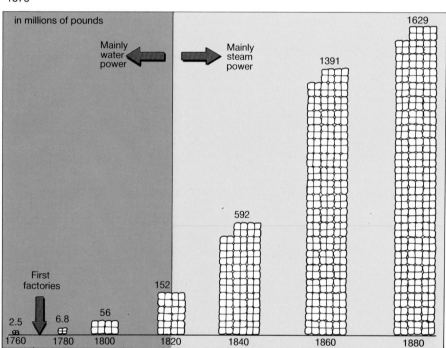

in millions of pounds

Mainly water power ← → Mainly steam power

First factories

2.5 | 6.8 | 56 | 152 | 592 | 1391 | 1629
1760 | 1780 | 1800 | 1820 | 1840 | 1860 | 1880

Source 83 Manchester, about 1850, a contemporary print

The industrial revolution in Britain: energy and the factory system

The industrial revolution began in Britain in the cotton industry. At first it depended on well-tried sources of energy like horses, wind power and water power.

- *What sources of energy were used in transporting the cotton in the days of William Strutt, and in working it in his mill?*

- *What were the earliest dates in history at which each of these might have been used?*

- *What made the factory system develop when it did, and not earlier?*

Steam-powered factories could be made as large as the owners wanted. They could also be built quite close to each other. This led to the building of densely-packed industrial areas.

- *Why had it not been possible to pack factories and mills closely together in the days of water-power?*

- *What other advantages do you think steam-powered mills had over water-powered mills?*

- *What disadvantages did they have?*

Energy for transport

An industrial city like Manchester would have been impossible without good transport. Coal, iron raw materials like cotton, building materials for houses, food for people – all these had to be carried to the towns. Finished products had to be carried away for sale all over the world.

Naturally these things were at first carried by time-tested methods: sailing ships and horse drawn barges and wagons. But once reliable steam engines came into use several people tried to use them to replace horses.

Railways
Richard Trevithick was a Cornishman who during the 1790s began to build engines with far more steam pressure than Watt would allow. His engines were just as powerful as Watt's but very much smaller. They were small enough to be used as locomotives – to move along pulling a load behind them. But they were so heavy that they broke the rails, and Trevithick lost interest.

In the years 1812–30 many other people experimented with stronger rails and lighter locomotives. They were mainly colliery engineers from North-East England, like George Stephenson. With his son Robert he finally solved all the problems and proved the success of steam locomotives in 1830 on the Liverpool and Manchester Railway.

- *Why do certain areas of the map have a lot of branch lines?*

- *What other goods needed to be cheap and plentiful before railways could spread as rapidly as this?*

Steamships
The first really successful steam-boat was made by Robert Fulton and ran on the East River, New York in 1807. It used one of Boulton and Watt's engines.

Although boats like Fulton's worked well on rivers and for short sea journeys, they were no use for ocean crossings. For these a ship had to carry enough coal to keep its engine running for weeks and still have room for cargo or passengers. It had to be reliable even in storms.

During the fifty years from 1840 to 1890 these problems were solved and steam ships took over from sail on most main sea trading routes.

The coming of steamships was very important. In the sixteenth century the Europeans in their new ocean-going sailing ships had begun to link the whole world together into a single trading system. In the nineteenth century they used the steamship to complete this. By 1880 people in England ate bread made from wheat grown in Canada. Coal from Wales was used to run trains in Brazil. Peasants in China wore cloth woven in Manchester.

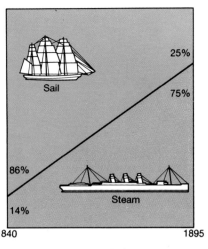

Sail *versus* steam, 1840–95

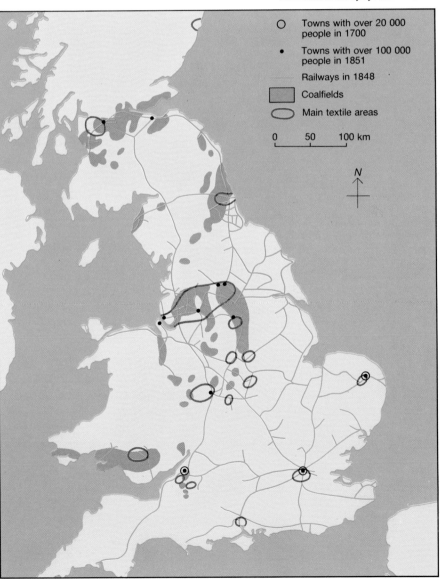

The British railway system in 1848

○ Towns with over 20 000 people in 1700

• Towns with over 100 000 people in 1851

— Railways in 1848

▨ Coalfields

⬭ Main textile areas

0   50   100 km

N

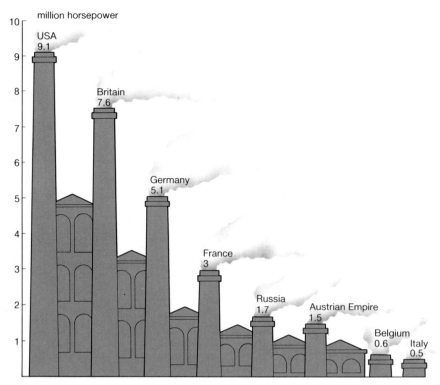

million horsepower

USA 9.1
Britain 7.6
Germany 5.1
France 3
Russia 1.7
Austrian Empire 1.5
Belgium 0.6
Italy 0.5

Steam power in 1880. No other country had over 0.5 million horsepower. The world total (34.15 million horsepower) was twenty times as much as in 1840

'The place for smoke to come out'

'Americans burn coal here'

'This (bell) is the one to hit when running'

Source 85 The US Navy Commander Perry gave this locomotive to the Shogun in 1854. From a drawing by a Japanese artist at the time

The industrial revolution spreads to other countries

The new railways and steamships spread rapidly in Europe and the USA. By 1840, only ten years after the opening of the Liverpool and Manchester Railway, the locomotive firm Robert Stephenson and Co. had sold engines to three railways in France, one in Belgium, one in Austria, four in Germany, one in Italy, one in Russia and six in the USA. At the same time these countries were building iron works, and cotton factories, sinking coal mines, and making increasing use of steam power.

- *The steam engine was first developed in Britain. The other countries on the chart above were the next ones to use it. Why did it spread first to those countries and not to others?*

- *What goods would they first need to have in cheap and plentiful supply?*

- *What ideas would their businessmen need to have?*

- *What knowledge and skill would their craftsmen need?*

People in countries like Germany and the USA welcomed the industrial revolution. The new sources of energy and the new methods of manufacture were used to make these countries richer and to improve life for many of their people. But people living in the low energy countries came face to face with the dark side of the energy revolution. This was because the high energy nations were now much more powerful in war.

Source 84 An early ironworks at Berlin. A painting by E. Biermann, 1847

Energy for war

Countries whose people had learned how to use the steam engine and the improved methods of making iron could make bigger and more accurate weapons. They could make them in larger numbers and they could use steamships or railways to carry them to a point of battle. These countries could deliver a much heavier punch than any others.

Source 86 British gunboat defeats the Chinese

The Nemesis was the first iron steamer that passed the Cape of Good Hope, and the first that appeared in China . . . When within 500 yards (of the Chinese war junks) the Nemesis commenced a heavy fire of shot and shell on the four largest, which was returned by them. The first Congreve rocket fired by her took terrific effect – blowing up one of the largest junks with all her crew. The others being silenced she then sent off her boats in company with those from (other British ships). Junk after junk was boarded and set fire to. The whole, 11 in number, blew up as the fire reached their magazines, and thus were completely destroyed . . . One shot only struck the Nemesis. The others fell short or went over. (*Illustrated London News* 12 November 1842)

Source 87 The illustration which accompanied Source 86 in the *Illustrated London News*

In 1842 The Chinese Government agreed to give Hong Kong to Britain. British merchants were allowed to trade freely in China and given special privileges in certain Chinese ports. When there were further problems in 1859 a joint British and French army was landed. marched to Peking and burned the Emperor's palace. China had been 'opened up'.

■ *What were the various ways, direct and indirect, in which the steam engine made these events possible!*

Source 88 An exhibit by Krupp of Essen, Germany at the Paris Exhibition of 1867, from a contemporary German magazine

Source 89 Boulton and Watt's Soho works, about 1850, from a contemporary engraving

Source 90 From W Fordyce: *A History of Coal, Coke and Coalfields, 1860*

Source 91 How a French artist, G. Doré, saw London in 1860

Life and work in industrial Britain

■ *How much of the work of the men in the middle picture could be taken over by the steam engine?*

Source 92 Sheffield smoke and grime

Sheffield is one of the dirtiest and most smoky towns I ever saw. There are a quantity of small forges without tall chimneys. The town is also very hilly, and the smoke ascends the streets instead of leaving them. It is usual for the children to wash before they go to bed, but not universal. Their bodies imbibe continual dust and grime. One cannot be long in the town without breathing in soot, which accumulates in the lungs. Its baneful effects are experienced by all who are not accustomed to it. There are, however, numbers of people in Sheffield who think the smoke healthy.
(Report of Parliamentary Committee, 1843)

Source 93 Pollution in Manchester

The river Irk, black with the refuse of dye-works erected on its banks, receives excrement . . . from some sewers in this portion of the town, the drainage of the gas-works and filth of the most pernicious character from bone-works, tanneries etc . . . pursuing the course of the river on the other side of Ducie Bridge, other tanneries, size-manufactories and tripe houses occur. The parish burial ground occupies one side of the stream and a series of courts of the most singular and unhealthy character the other.
(Dr. J.P. Kay: *The Moral and Physical Condition of the Working Class in Manchester*, 1832)

■ *The sources above show some of the problems of industrial towns.*

■ *Which of these problems were directly due to the use of steam engines?*

■ *Which were indirectly due to steam power? Which had nothing to do with it?*

Source 94 Factory work is easy

I have seen tens of thousands of both sexes, many of them too feeble to get their bread by any of the former modes of industry, earning enough without perspiring at a single pore. They are screened meanwhile from the summer's sun and the winter's frost, in apartments more airy and healthy than those in which our fashionable aristocracies assemble. In these spacious halls the kindly power of steam summons around him his willing menials. He assigns to each the regulated task, substituting for painful muscular effort on their part, the energies of his own gigantic arm. He demands in return only attention and dexterity.

(Andrew Ure: *Philosophy of Manufacture*, 1835)

- *Which of sources 93 and 94 is likely to be the more reliable?*

- *What other evidence would be needed to make a balanced judgement of conditions of work in factories in the nineteenth century?*

- *Would it make any difference to conditions of work whether the factory was powered by steam or water?*

- *Why was discipline and good time-keeping more important in a large factory than it had been for workers before the industrial revolution?*

Source 95

RULES
TO BE OBSERVED
By the Hands Employed in
THIS MILL.

RULE 1. All the Overlookers shall be on the premises first and last.

2. Any Person coming too late shall be fined as follows:—for 5 minutes 2d, 10 minutes 4d, and 15 minutes 6d, &c.

3. For any Bobbins found on the floor 1d for each Bobbin.

4. For single Drawing, Slubbing, or Roving 2d for each single end.

5. For Waste on the floor 2d.

6. For any Oil wasted or spilled on the floor 2d each offence, besides paying for the value of the Oil.

7. For any broken Bobbins, they shall be paid for according to their value, and if there is any difficulty in ascertaining the guilty party, the same shall be paid for by the whole using such Bobbins.

8. Any person neglecting to Oil at the proper times shall be fined 2d.

9. Any person leaving their Work and found Talking with any of the other workpeople shall be fined 2d for each offence.

10. For every Oath or insolent language, 3d for the first offence, and if repeated they shall be dismissed.

11. The Machinery shall be swept and cleaned down every meal time.

12. All persons in our employ shall serve Four Weeks' Notice before leaving their employ; but L. WHITAKER & SONS, shall and will turn any person off without notice being given.

13. If two persons are known to be in one Necessary together they shall be fined 3d each; and if any Man or Boy go into the Women's Necessary he shall be instantly dismissed.

14. Any person wilfully or negligently breaking the Machinery, damaging the Brushes, making too much Waste, &c., they shall pay for the same to its full value.

15. Any person hanging anything on the Gas Pendants will be fined 2d.

16. The Masters would recommend that all their workpeople Wash themselves every morning, but they shall Wash themselves at least twice every week, Monday Morning and Thursday morning; and any found not washed will be fined 3d for each offence.

17. The Grinders, Drawers, Slubbers and Rovers shall sweep at least eight times in the day as follows, in the Morning at 7½, 9½, 11 and 12; and in the Afternoon at 1½, 2½, 3½, 4½ and 5½ o'clock; and to notice the Board hung up, when the black side is turned that is the time to sweep, and only quarter of an hour will be allowed for sweeping. The Spinners shall sweep as follows, in the Morning at 7½, 10 and 12; in the Afternoon at 3 and 5½ o'clock. Any neglecting to sweep at the time will be fined 2d for each offence.

18. Any persons found Smoking on the premises will be instantly dismissed.

19. Any person found away from their usual place of work, except for necessary purposes, or Talking with any one out of their own Alley will be fined 2d for each offence.

20. Any person bringing dirty Bobbins will be fined 1d for each Bobbin.

21. Any person wilfully damaging this Notice will be dismissed.

The Overlookers are strictly enjoined to attend to these Rules, and they will be responsible to the Masters for the Workpeople observing them.

WATER-FOOT MILL, NEAR HASLINGDEN,
SEPTEMBER, 1851.

J. Read, Printer, and Bookbinder, Haslingden.

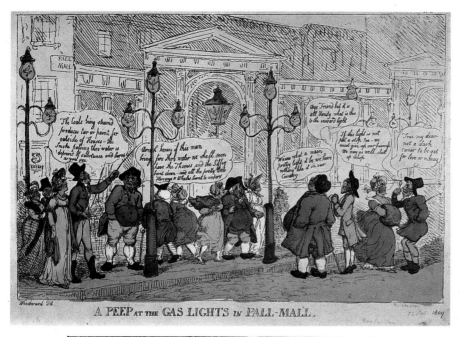

A PEEP AT THE GAS LIGHTS IN PALL-MALL.

The good Effects of CARBONIC GAS!!!

Coal gas used for lighting

In the new factories a working day of 12 to 14 hours was quite common. A mill-owner who had invested a great deal of capital in buildings and machinery always wanted to keep them in use for as many hours as possible. So artificial light was essential. Oil lamps and candles were used at first, but they are easily knocked over. They often set the whole mill on fire. Coal gas was a waste product of the coke-making process in the iron industry. At first it was just burned away. In 1791 a French inventor, Philippe Labon, developed a way of using it for lighting. But he was not able to get any support from rich investors.

In England William Murdock had been working independently along similar lines. He had little difficulty in persuading his employers, Boulton and Watt, to start making gas 'retorts' and burners. In 1804 they sold their first set to a large Salford cotton mill.

The industrial town with its houses, factories and public buildings tightly packed together had one advantage. A fuel like gas could be supplied to a whole area or even a whole town from one gas-works. The man who first saw this possibility was a German immigrant called F.A. Winser. He promised to, 'provide our streets and houses with light and heat ... as they are now supplied with water.' He claimed that his scheme would make a profit of £227 million! He was not succesful himself, but the company he started, the Gas, Light and Coke Company, had laid 26 miles of cast-iron gas mains by 1815. Gas companies were started in most of the other industrial towns during the next fifty years.

The open burners gave a yellow, often smoky light, but gas lighting was much cheaper and safer than candles or oil-lamps.

■ *Why did gas lighting first succeed in Britain rather than France?*

■ *Not everyone welcomed gas lighting. Why was this?*

Source 97 The March of Intellect, a cartoon by an unidentified artist, 1829

Source 98 Steam-powered boots. An 1820 cartoon by R. Seymour

MARCH of INTELLECT

Tomorrow's world, yesterday

About the year 1800 the idea of 'progress' became fashionable, and many guesses were made about the future.

Source 99 Steam aeroplanes

Soon shall thy arm, unconquered Steam,
  afar
Drag the slow barge or drive the rapid car;
Or on wide-waving wings expanded bear
The flying chariot through the fields of air.
Fair crews triumphant, leaning from above,
Shall wave their fluttering kerchiefs as they
  move;
Or warrior bands alarm the gaping crowd,
And armies shrink beneath the shadowy
  cloud.
(From *The Botanic Garden* by Erasmus Darwin, 1791. Darwin was a friend of James Watt.)

■ *In what ways were these guesses right and in what ways were they wrong?*

■ *Why should there be so many guesses about the future in this period?*

Source 100
Air-um Scare-um Travelling, 1843, by G. Cruikshank

Changes and developments 1500–1875

By 1875 Britain and a few other countries in Western Europe and North America had completed the 'second energy revolution'. In Britain about 4 tonnes of coal were used in a year for each man woman and child. (In 1983 we used the equivalent of 5.3 tonnes each.)

In these coal-rich countries a new industrial way of life was being set up. It depended on coal and steam.

Much work even in the rich countries was still done by animals and man-power, as well as by wind and water mills. But the new prime mover, the steam engine, could turn heat into power. So the Europeans and North Americans had begun to tap the reserves of energy stored up in fossil fuels.

As well as using this power to run their factories, they had applied it to transport. Their ships and railways held the world together in an iron grip.

Nine out of ten of the world's people still lived a low energy way of life. The Europeans had used their superior ships, guns and horses to seize control of large empires in the sixteenth century. Now, with railways and steamships and bigger guns than ever, nothing could stand in their way.

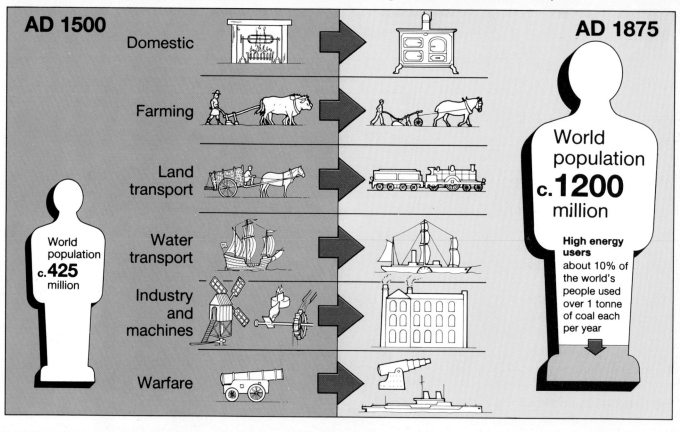

AD 1500

Domestic

Farming

Land transport

Water transport

Industry and machines

Warfare

World population c.**425** million

AD 1875

World population c.**1200** million

High energy users about 10% of the world's people used over 1 tonne of coal each per year

5

High energy civilisation 1875 to the present

Electricity: energy you can switch on and off

Until about 1875 most of the new ways of using energy were developed by practical men like Thomas Newcomen or George Stephenson, who knew very little science. James Watt was a scientist as well as an engineer, but this was very unusual.

The position with electricity was quite different. It was developed entirely by scientists through experiments and for a long time it was was of little practical use. Many scientific problems had to be solved before useful electrical machines could be made.

Scientists investigate electricity

Scientists had been interested in electricity since the sixteenth century. But they had only been able to make sparks and flashes, which were hard to study.

In 1800 the Italian Alessandro Volta found out how to make a battery that produced a steady current of electricity. This made research much easier.

In 1809 the British Sir Humphrey Davy used a large battery to make a brilliant electric light. But this light was far too expensive to be of any practical use.

Michael Faraday used the ideas of Davy and others to work out many of the basic principles of electricity. Between 1821 and 1831 he showed how an electric generator and an electric motor could be made.

Faraday was far too interested in his scientific research to spend time making generators and motors. Other people made them, but for 40 years none were of much practical use. Electricity was still mainly of scientific interest.

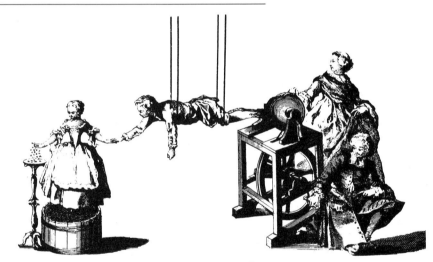

Source 101 A demonstration about 1750 by Dr W. Watson. As the man cranked the wheel, it picked up a static electric charge from the woman's hand and transferred it to the feet of the boy suspended on silk ropes. The charge then went to the girl standing on an insulating tub of dried pitch. Her hand attracted chaff from the table

Electric current 'arcs' across the gap

The carbons burn white hot and give off intense light

Metal holders

Wires to battery

Sir Humphrey Davy's electric arc

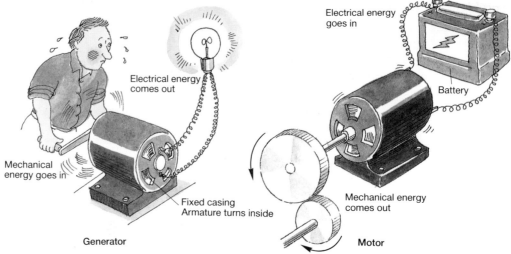

Source 102 The first working telegraph, made by William Cooke and Charles Wheatstone, London 1837. A telegraph like this was installed on a stretch of the new Great Western Railway near Paddington station in 1838. There were five keys which made the needles point to the letters of the alphabet. The needles on a similar board at the other end of the line did the same

Electrical energy comes out

Mechanical energy goes in

Fixed casing
Armature turns inside

Generator

Electrical energy goes in

Battery

Mechanical energy comes out

Motor

The difference between an electric generator and an electric motor

The only important practical use of electricity before 1875 was the telegraph. This was because it used only tiny amounts of electricity to carry information which might save life or be worth millions of pounds.

In the 1840s, '50s and '60s, as the telegraph spread, a new sort of craftsman came into being – the telegraph operator. He had to know some science, and he also had to have the same sort of practical skill with electrical machines as men like Stephenson or Newcomen had with steam engines.

One young telegraph operator on the American railroads was Thomas A. Edison. Men like Edison were to play an important part in bringing electricity into widespread use in the years after 1875.

Electric light

Source 103 Football match between Wanderers v. Clapham Rovers on 4 November 1878, lit by the new electric light at Kennington Oval. From the *Illustrated Sporting and Dramatic News*

Source 104 Almost as clear as noonday

On Monday night in Sheffield a crowd of nearly 30 000 people gathered at Bramhall Lane grounds to watch a football match played under the electric light. The match was played by two teams belonging to the Sheffield Football Association. It commenced at half past seven o'clock. The electric light was thrown from four lamps 30 feet (9 m.) from the ground. The rays lighted nearly the whole of the ground, the players being seen almost as clear as at noonday. The brilliance of the light, however, dazzled the players and sometimes caused strange blunders.

(The Electrician 1878)

These lights were made possible by a new and much improved generator, invented in 1871 by the Belgian Z.T. Gramme. Cheap and reliable electric current was now available. From about 1875 'arc lights' like these, working on the principles Davy had used in 1809, began to be used for outdoor lighting. They gave a brilliant light but were too large and dangerous to use indoors.

The problem of indoor electric light

As early as 1820 people had suggested making an electric light inside a glass container. In the years 1879–81 three men, working independently of each other made successful light bulbs.

■ *The idea of the light bulb was already 60 years old in 1880. Why should three men separately invent successful ones at more or less the same time?*

Most industrial towns in 1880 had a well-established public system of gas mains and gas lighting. The electrical engineers now began to set up rival systems of public electricity supply. Edison was the most determined of these engineers. In 1882 he built the world's first power stations selling electricity to private houses. One of his stations was in London and one in New York.

These early electric light systems were expensive. Bulbs cost £1.25 each, (about a week's wages for a working man). They were not very reliable. Most people kept to gas, oil-lamps or candles.

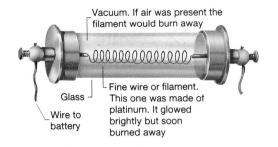

Vacuum. If air was present the filament would burn away

Glass

Wire to battery

Fine wire or filament. This one was made of platinum. It glowed brightly but soon burned away

W. de la Rue's lamp, 1820. The filament was made of platinum. It glowed brightly but soon burned away. The problems were to make a high vacuum inside the glass and a filament that would not burn away

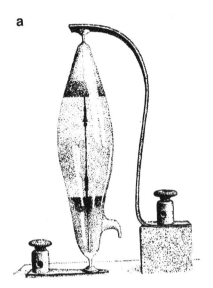

a

b

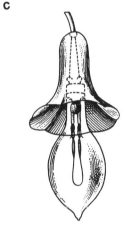

c

Source 105

a) J. Swan's lamp, 1878 – the first one demonstrated in public.

b) T. Edison's lamp, 1881.

c) St. G. Lane-Fox's lamp, 1881

Source 106 *Left*: The gas mantle as used in this lamp was invented in 1885

Source 107

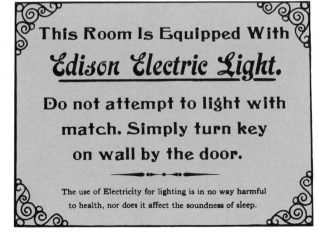

More powerful generators and cheaper electricity

To work efficiently and to produce cheap electricity, generators needed to spin faster than the steam engines of the 1880s could drive them. Two answers were found to this problem.

1 Water power makes a come-back

In France there was plenty of water power and very little coal. So when the steam engine took over from water power in England the French continued to use watermills. In the 1830s B. Fourneyron, engineer in a French iron works, invented the 'water turbine'.

In the 1880s water turbines were found to be an ideal way of driving generators. In 1895 the Niagara Falls Power Company used two Fourneyron-type turbines with a power of 1100 hp to drive generators. This was the first large hydro-electric station.

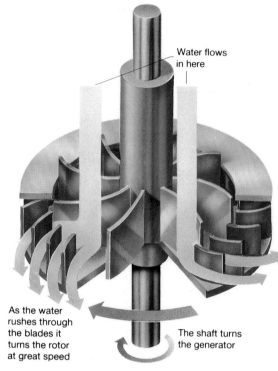

Water flows in here

As the water rushes through the blades it turns the rotor at great speed

The shaft turns the generator

A water turbine was a very precisely-made machine, which wasted hardly any of the power of falling water. It spun round like a whirlpool, and could produce much more power than a mill-wheel, and turned much faster

A turbo-generator

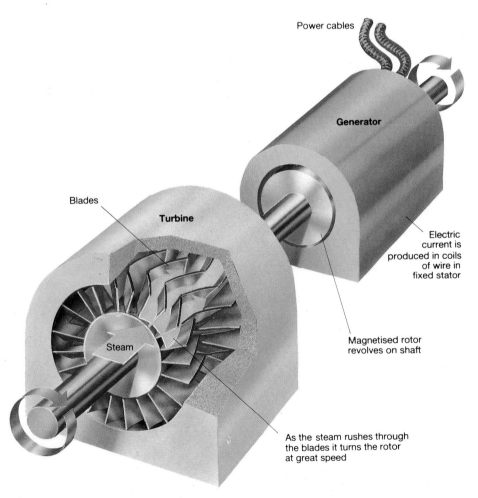

Power cables

Generator

Blades

Turbine

Steam

Electric current is produced in coils of wire in fixed stator

Magnetised rotor revolves on shaft

As the steam rushes through the blades it turns the rotor at great speed

2 Steam turbines

In the cities, where electric lighting was most needed, there was often little water-power. So an improved steam engine was needed if electric generators were to work efficiently. In 1884 the British engineer C.A. Parsons invented the steam turbine. This was the most important improvement in the steam engine since James Watt's rotary engine. Like Watt, Parsons was a scientist as well as an engineer. He put together knowledge of steam, worked out by Watt and others, and knowledge of turbines, worked out by Fourneyron. Inside Parsons' machine there were no pistons rushing up and down. Instead there was a 'rotor' spinning round like a whirlpool.

Parsons also designed a special generator which would work efficiently at the speed that best suited his turbines. The first power station to use his machines was opened in 1890 at Newcastle. Since about 1900 all power stations anywhere in the world have been powered either by steam turbines or by water turbines.

Two types of electric current: the 'battle of the systems'

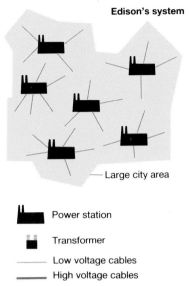

Edison's system

Large city area

Power station

Transformer

Low voltage cables

High voltage cables

Tesla's system

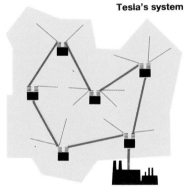

Near to supply of coal or water power

Generators can be designed to produce two types of electric current, *alternating* (a.c.) and *direct* (d.c.).

By 1890 Thomas Edison had planned and built several small power stations to distribute d.c current over short distances. But his rival, George Westinghouse, employed a clever young Serbian electrical engineer, Nikola Tesla. In 1888 Tesla designed an a.c. motor, and went on to develop a complete a.c. system.

From 1890 until about 1900 there was some doubt about which system would succeed. Edison fought bitterly for d.c. His chief argument was that a.c. was more dangerous. Some of his friends tried to prove this by persuading New York State to use electricity for execution, and to use Westinghouse's alternating current.

Source 108 Far worse than hanging. Kemmler's death proves an awful spectacle
The electric current had to be turned on twice before the deed was fully accomplished.
(*New York Times*, 7 August 1890)

Despite Edison's arguments, Westinghouse and Tesla won the 'battle of the systems'. In 1895 they were given the contract for the Niagara power station. It supplied power to the city of Buffalo, 36 kilometres away.

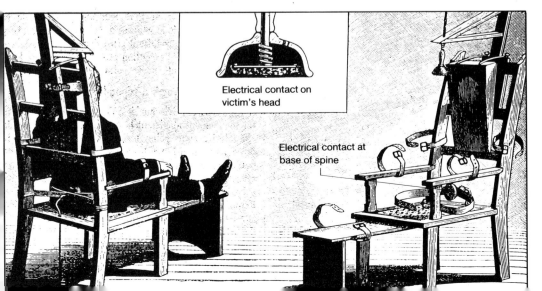

Electrical contact on victim's head

Electrical contact at base of spine

Source 109 The electric chair, 1890, from a contemporary drawing

Battersea power station, 1934

National systems of power supply

One big station was far more efficient than many small ones. So the coming of long distance transmission of electricity led to bigger power stations.

There was one main reason why a.c. won the 'battle of the system'. Using Tesla's system, power could be taken from areas where there was plenty of coal or water power, to areas where there was little. Also if there was a power failure in one town, electricity could easily be switched into the area from somewhere else. This led governments to set up large electricity distribution systems, fed by many power stations.

In Britain the government set up in 1926 a 'Central Electricity Board' to organise and control a national grid or transmission system. The system was completed in 1935.

Most other advanced countries did the same. In the twentieth century people have come to depend on electricity, just as in the Stone Age they had come to depend on fire. Day and night, seven days a week, people needed to switch on the light, to travel by tram or underground railway, or to keep machines running in factory or hospital. There has to be a completely reliable system of distributing electricity. In a small country with room for only one grid system, the government took control. In some countries, like Britain in 1947, the government took over ownership of the power stations as well. In others like the USA, they left the ownership of power stations in the hands of private firms. but set up government bodies to control them.

■ *Can you think of other examples in history when governments or other powerful groups have tried to control a source of energy?*

■ *Which people or groups of people might disapprove of this control?*

Electricity pylons. Pylons carry the cables which transmit high voltage current over long distances

The world's largest power stations

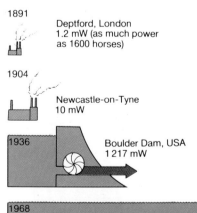

1891
Deptford, London
1.2 mW (as much power as 1600 horses)

1904
Newcastle-on-Tyne
10 mW

1936
Boulder Dam, USA
1 217 mW

1968
Krasnoyarsk Dam, USSR
6 096 mW

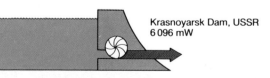
1984
Itaip
Bra
12

New uses for electricity

By 1900 the main problems of generating and transmitting electricity had been solved. As electricity became cheap and reliable it found many other uses as well as lighting. It could be used in very small amounts, as in a telephone or a clock. It could be used in very large amounts, as in an electric furnace making steel. It could be turned on and off at will. It could be led in quite small cables to the top of a tall building or to the bottom of a coal mine. It made no smell or smoke, except at the power station.

The dates given in this diagram are those at which electricity was first used in practice for each purpose. In many cases it took a long time for it to come into widespread use.

■ Which of the tasks shown below were new and could only be done by electricity?

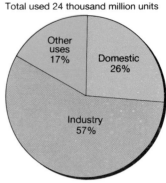

1940
Total used 24 thousand million units

Other uses 17%
Domestic 26%
Industry 57%

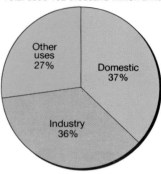

1980
Total used 192 thousand million units

Other uses 27%
Domestic 37%
Industry 36%

The uses of electricity in Britain. 1940 and 1980

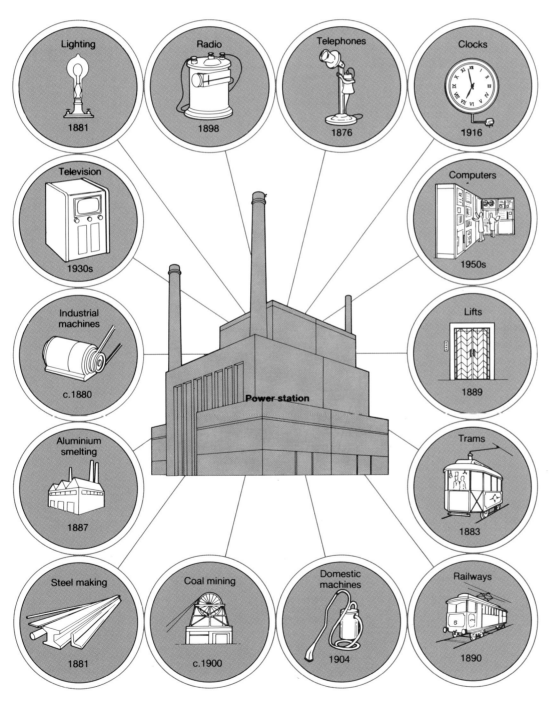

Lighting 1881
Radio 1898
Telephones 1876
Clocks 1916
Television 1930s
Computers 1950s
Industrial machines c.1880
Lifts 1889
Aluminium smelting 1887
Trams 1883
Steel making 1881
Coal mining c.1900
Domestic machines 1904
Railways 1890
Power station

World aluminium production

	tonnes
1875	2.5
1900	7300
1980	35 000 000

Percentage of British coal worked by powered machinery underground

	% cut	% conveyed
1900	1.5	0
1950	80	80

Source 110 A 1909 advertisement

Source 111 An illustration to a science fiction story written in 1896.

■ *Electric trams and motor cars were already in use at this date. Why should the author invent this unlikely beast?*

Source 112 An electric tram, Portsmouth, 1935

An advantage and a disadvantage

One advantage of electricity is that it can be transmitted over long distances. Previously bulky fuels and heavy machines had to be moved to the place where work was to be done. Now energy could be produced in one place and used in another. The massive power of a steam engine or a water turbine in the power station can be led along a wire only a few centimetres thick to the place where it is needed.

Most industrial cities set up electric tramways systems about the year 1900. Electric tramways made good use of the power carried along their overhead cables. But the trams could never move away from the power cables.

Number of electric trams in Great Britain

1898	1000
1910	12000
1926	15000

By 1926 buses using petrol or diesel engines were beginning to take over. They could travel on any road, and they needed no power cables. So they were cheaper. By 1960 the Blackpool trams were the only ones left in Britain.

Source 113 The end of the industrial city?

England in future, instead of being spoiled by densely populated industrial centres, might be covered by cottages extending for miles over the present rural district. The factory hands instead of having to work under the shafting in factories, should be able by the electrical transmission of power to work in their own cottage homes. This is the future which lies before electrical engineers . . .

(R.E.B. Crompton, a leading British electrical engineer, 1900)

■ *Has any part of Crompton's dream come true? Is it likely to do so in the future?*

The fossil fuels in the high energy world

It was coal which made the high energy world possible, and coal has continued to be very important in the twentieth century. World output has gone on rising steadily. In some old mining areas output has fallen as mines have been exhausted. But new mines have been opened elsewhere.

The new coal field at Selby, one of the biggest in the world, was started in 1976. It is expected to produce 10 million tonnes a year by 1990.

In the twentieth century two other fossil fuels, oil and natural gas have begun to compete with coal.

Source 114 From the National Coal Board's press statement, 1976

The early use of oil

Oil has been used for lighting since the Stone Age.

In some places, like Iran, mineral oil seeped out of the ground, and was used in lamps. In others, people used olive oil or animal oils. Whales and seals were hunted for their oil by seafaring people.

With the coming of the industrial city, lighting in streets and factories became important. In towns, especially in countries like Britain where there was plenty of coal, gas made from coal solved the problem. But in other areas there was a great demand for oil.

Source 115 *Left*: The whale blubber was heated to extract the oil. Wooden barrels were then used to carry it to market. Oil is still measured in 'barrels'. From Olaus Magnus, *History of the Western Peoples*, Rome, 1555

Source 116 A stone lamp from France, about 20 000 BC, and how it was used

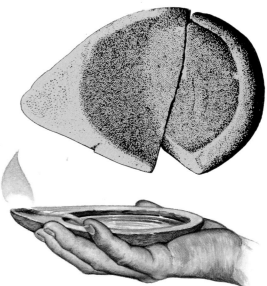

The first oil fields

It was the Americans, in the 1850s and 1860s, who first learned to tap oil deep underground. Before that this oil was just a nuisance which seeped into wells drilled for water or for brine (needed to make salt). The idea of drilling for oil first occurred to a group of business men in 1854. They founded the 'Pennsylvania Rock Oil Company'. Before they spent very much money they sent a sample of crude oil to Professor Silliman of Yale University. He analysed it and saw that it could be used to make paraffin for lamps.

Source 117 The company's engineer, Colonel Drake (in top hat). Drake struck oil on 27 August 1859. Photograph taken 1861

Source 118 Below: Within a few years the area looked like this. Benninghof Run, Pennsylvania, in 1865

Source 119 A valuable raw material
In conclusion, gentlemen, it appears to me that your company have in their possession a raw material from which, by a simple and not expensive process, they may manufacture many valuable products.
(Professor Silliman's report, 16 April 1855)

In America several 'gold rushes' took place. Now an 'oil rush' began.

Source 120 The first oil rush
(a) The Funk well . . . was struck in June 1861 and commenced flowing to the astonishment of all the oil-borers in the neighbourhood, at the rate of 250 barrels a day. The oil continued flowing . . . for fifteen months, and then stopped, but not before Funk became a rich man . . . Down on the Tarr farm, the Philips well burst forth with a stream of two thousand barrels daily. The Empire well, close to the Funk, suddenly burst forth with its three thousand barrels daily. The owners were bewildered . ... The supply was already in advance of the demand . . . The price fell to twenty cents a barrel, then to fifteen, then to ten. Coopers (who made wooden barrels) would sell barrels for cash only, and refused to take their pay in oil.
(b) I learned that the Farrell well, at Titusville, produced more oil than eight hundred whaleships had collected in a year at New Bedford.
(E. Morris: *Derrick and Drill*, New York, 1865)

Source 121 Oil is indispensable
From Maine to California oil lights our dwellings, lubricates our machinery, and is indispensable in numerous departments of arts, manufactures and domestic life. To be deprived of it now would be setting us back a whole cycle of civilisation
(J.Bone: *Petroleum and Petroleum Wells*, Philadelphia, 1865)

- *Why did the modern oil industry begin in the USA, and not in some other country?*

- *Why did it begin around the middle of the nineteenth century and not at some other time?*

Source 123 Transport of oil, Pennsylvania, 1871, a contemporary drawing

The growth of the oil business

The journey of the oil from the well to the lamps in which people burned it was long and complicated.

Refineries, special rail wagons and later on tankers and pipe-lines, all cost a great deal to build or to buy. But once the money had been spent far fewer workers were needed than in coal mining. So once the capital had been invested fortunes could be made out of oil. The American J.D. Rockefeller saw this first. He left the chancy business of drilling for oil to others. Instead he set up refineries and bought those built by other people. He also tried to get control of oil transport. By the time he was 33, in 1872, his company, the Standard Oil Company, owned 90 per cent of American refineries and all the oil wagons on the Pennsylvania Railroad.

Source 122 **Trade with us – or else . . .**
The officers of the Standard Oil Company made no bones about it at all. They said 'if you don't sell your oil to us, it will be valueless'.
(Frank Rockefeller, speaking to a Committee of Congress, 1876)

■ *Why would the oil of the other producers be valueless if they refused to sell to Rockefeller?*

By 1900 Standard Oil controlled 80 per cent of the trade in oil and Rockefeller was the richest man in the world.

From oil well to oil lamp. The process of production in the nineteenth century

Ships like these cost millions of pounds to build but can carry 200 000 tonnes of oil half way round the world for about £100 a tonne. To transport a pound's worth of oil in this way costs only 2p

Source 124 An early oil tanker, 1917

World-wide trade in oil

Oil wells were soon developed in other countries and oil has since been discovered in many parts of the world. Since the 1950s methods have even been invented for getting it from under the sea bed.

But most countries in the world have no oil of their own. So as soon as oil became important a world oil trade began. The first cargo of oil crossed the Atlantic, packed in wooden barrels, in 1861. By 1890 there were about 50 oil tankers, ships specially built to carry oil.

Below: A pipeline being laid down in Scotland. Pipelines can cost £100 000 a kilometre to build but can carry oil for hundreds of kilometres, adding only 8 per cent to the sale price of oil

An oil rig in the North Sea

Another way of moving oil over long distances is by pipe-line. The first ones were built in America and Russia in the 1870s.

Oil becomes the world's leading fossil fuel

In the 1960s the world began to get more of its energy from oil than from coal. We could call the nineteenth and early twentieth centuries the 'Age of Coal' and the later twentieth century the 'Age of Oil'.

Why did oil take over? It has three great advantages:

1 There is twice as much energy in a tonne of oil as in a tonne of coal. This makes it possible for cars and aeroplanes to carry their own fuel with them. Coal would be too heavy.

2 Oil is much cheaper and easier to get than coal. Once oil is struck it gushes out of some wells under its own pressure. The oil-well at Spindletop in Texas in 1901 produced over a hundred thousand barrels a day. It would have taken 37000 miners working hard for a day to produce enough coal to provide the same amount of energy.

3 Oil is a liquid, so it can be moved easily by tanker or pipeline. There is no need for industries using oil to stay near to coal fields.

Ever since nomadic hunters settled down into permanent agricultural settlements people have had to transport fuel from a distance. Fuels like wood charcoal and coal are awkward to carry. So industries such as iron-working which use a lot of fuel had to be near to forests or coal mines. During the 'Age of Coal' the rich industrial countries were those with a supply of coal near at hand.

In the 'Age of Oil' things are different. The rich industrial countries have been able to fetch oil from the other side of the world without adding too much to its cost.

- *What new dangers might this cause for the rich industrial countries?*

- *What problems might it cause for poor countries in which oil has been discovered?*

Source 125 The petrol-engined horse: invented in France in 1897.

■ *Why?*

Source 126 A modern artist's impression of Gottlieb Daimler's motor cycle; the first effective motor vehicle using an internal combustion engine, 1885

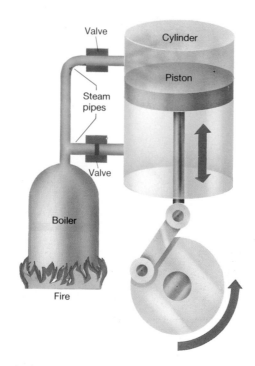

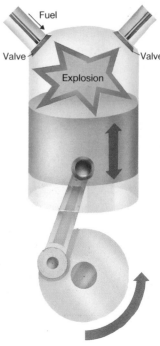

The cycle of the steam engine (*left*), and the internal combustion engine (*above*)

Engines using oil

Until about 1900 most oil was used for lighting. But it was such a convenient fuel that it was already beginning to be used in other ways.

Oil could be burned instead of coal in a steam engine. An oil-burning battle-ship could go faster, travel further and carry more guns. By 1920 20 per cent of the world's ships were oil-powered, and by 1945 74 per cent. A much more important development was however, the 'internal combustion engine'.

The motor car
Ever since the coming of steam, people had tried to make a 'horseless carriage'. Using oil as fuel, some quite successful steam cars were made in the 1890s. But the final answer was a new type of engine, which was much lighter than the steam engine.

This is known as the 'internal combustion engine' because the fuel is burned inside the cylinder and not in a separate furnace. The first successful one was made by a German, N.A. Otto in 1878. It used gas made from coal as a fuel. It had to be connected to a gas main, so it was no use for vehicles.

In the 1880s and 90s several inventors, mainly in France, Germany and the USA successfully adapted the Otto engine to work with oil. It worked best with the very light and inflammable part of the oil which we call petrol. In the nineteenth century petrol had been an unwanted by-product of the oil refineries. In the twentieth century it became their best seller.

■ *Why was the motor car developed at this time?*

■ *Why was the motor car first widely successful in the USA?*

Source 127 It was in the USA that the motor car first became widely used. Henry Ford's Model T was the first mass produced car. It was cheap and reliable. It could go nearly anywhere. Between 1908 and 1928 Ford made 15 million of them.

An engine for heavy vehicles

In 1897 the German engineer Rudolf Diesel invented an internal combustion engine specially suited to heavy vehicles. It used much less fuel than a petrol engine, and gave higher power at low speeds. It also used a much less refined fuel, which was cheaper. By the 1930s most new vehicles in transport and industry had diesel engines.

Some modern uses of the diesel engine

Source 128 Old and new forms of energy. The Wrights' plane in France, 1909

automobile manufacturers could build one light enough by using more aluminium than in the regular output. On 3 December 1902 Wilbur sent letters to a number of manufacturers. Most of the companies replied that they were too busy to undertake such a special order. There is reason to suspect the companies may have got wind of the purpose to which the motor would be put. If a company provided a motor for a so-called flying-machine it could hurt their business prestige. It might look as if they considered human flight a possibility.

Finally the brothers decided that they would have to build their motor themselves. (F.C. Kelly: *The Wright Brothers*, 1944)

■ *Which developments in the history of energy made the Wrights' flight possible?*

In the 1930s a new type of aero-engine, the gas turbine, was invented independently in Britain and Germany. It combined the principles of the internal combustion engine with those of the steam turbine. It produced about twice as much power from the same amount of fuel as previous aero-engines.

Engines for aeroplanes

Earlier prime movers like water mills or steam engines had been adapted to drive many different machines. It was the same with the internal combustion engine.

Source 130 The first aero engine

The Wrights wanted a motor to produce at least eight horsepower and to weigh not more than 20 pounds (9 kilos) per horsepower. Perhaps one of the

A gas turbine

Fuel is injected into the combustion chamber

This fan compresses the air

Turbine: as the hot gases rush through the blades they turn the rotor at great speed

Jet of exhaust gas drives the plane forward

Source 129 *Above*: A Messerschmidt 262, the first successful jet fighter, 1944

A Boeing 707, the first commercially successful jet airliner, 1958. It cut the flying time between New York and Paris in half. Jet engines made cheap air travel possible in the 1960s

Natural gas

The last of the fossil fuels to come into use was natural gas. As with oil, people had known for a long time that it would burn. Natural gas can be found with coal or oil, or on its own. To the early oil men it was a nuisance and they burnt it – 'flared it off'.

Before it can be of much use, natural gas must be stored under pressure or fed through a pressurised steel pipe. A method of welding pipes together to make this possible was not discovered until 1925. So enormous amounts were wasted. Gas pipe-lines were built in the USA and in the USSR in the 1940s and 1950s.

In 1959 a massive gas-field was found off the coast of the Netherlands. In the 1960s many more gas-fields were found in the North Sea. It was quite easy to change over the existing gas systems of countries like Britain to 'North Sea Gas'.

Drilling for gas is often done by the big oil companies, but in most countries the gas is sold through government-owned corporations like the British Gas Board. This gives the government some control over production and prices.

Source 131 Miners using a bamboo pipe to burn off dangerous gas from a coal mine. From a Chinese book printed in 1637

Left and below: A British gas rig in the North Sea, and a gas terminal and pipelines at Aberdeen

A gas flare

Nuclear power: a new form of energy

In 1896 Henri Becquerel, a French scientist, discovered that the element uranium is 'radioactive' – it regularly gives off tiny bursts of energy. Until this time scientists had believed that matter and energy were two quite different things. By 1903 Ernest Rutherford had showed that in giving off energy uranium was actually changing into another element, and some of it was disappearing altogether. It looked as if matter was turning into energy!

In 1905 Albert Einstein suggested that all matter basically consisted of energy. He predicted in his famous equation '$e = mc^2$', that a very small amount of matter, m, would turn into an enormous amount of energy, e. At first people thought that this new form of energy could never be used.

Source 132 This energy can never be used: Einstein

'You're saying there's more horse-power in a lump of coal than in the whole Prussian cavalry,' complained Einstein's friends. 'If this were true, why hasn't it been noticed before?'

'If a man who is fabulously rich never spent or gave away a penny,' Einstein replied, 'then no-one could tell how rich he was or even if he had any money at all. It is the same with matter. So long as none of the energy is given off externally it cannot be observed.'

'And how do you propose to release all this hidden energy?'

'There is not the slightest indication that the energy will ever be obtainable,' said Einstein. 'It would mean that the atom would have to be shattered at will . . . We see the atom disintegrating only where Nature herself presents it.'

(P. Michelmore: *Portrait of Einstein* 1963)

■ *Why had this form of energy not been noticed earlier in history? What other form of energy was at first of interest only to scientists?*

The typical 'mushroom cloud' of a nuclear explosion

The atom bomb

In the 1930s physicists began to think that people might actually make use of the enormous energy inside the atom. In 1939 scientists in Germany, Denmark, France and Britain all came to believe that if enough of one special and very rare type of uranium (U235) was packed closely enough together, it might explode with about a million times the force of an ordinary bomb. The USA was well behind Europe in atomic physics, but several European scientists, especially Jews like Einstein, took refuge in the USA from the persecutions of Hitler.

Source 133 Einstein warns President Roosevelt

To F.D. Roosevelt,
President of the United States,
White House,
Washington D.C.   August 2nd. 1939
Sir,
Some recent work by E. Fermi and L. Szilard, leads me to suspect that the element uranium may be turned into a new and important source of energy in the near future . . . It may become possible to set up a nuclear chain reaction in a large mass of uranium, by which vast amounts of power would be generated.

This could also lead to the construction of bombs. A single bomb of this type, carried by boat and exploded in a port might well destroy the whole port together with some of the surrounding territory. However such bombs might very well prove too heavy for transportation by air.

In view of this situation you may think it desirable to (appoint) a person who has your confidence to speed up experimental work by providing funds.

I understand that Germany has actually stopped the sale of uranium.
Yours very truly,
Albert Einstein.

The USA did not join in the war against Hitler until December 1941, but President Roosevelt did provide enough money to keep nuclear research going in the universities. By 1941 it looked very likely that a nuclear bomb could be made within a few years, but it was clear that it would cost enormous amounts of time and money. In 1942 the US Government set up the 'Manhattan Project.' Its job was to make the bomb.

It was by far the biggest organisation of scientists and industry ever set up to carry out a single job. By 1945 it had made three bombs. On 6 August 1945 a US airforce B29 bomber dropped one of them on the Japanese city of Hiroshima. It killed 80 000 people immediately and another 60 000 within a year. Days later another bomb was dropped on the city of Nagasaki.

- *Why was this first use of nuclear energy developed in the USA?*

- *Would nuclear energy have been developed if there had been no war?*

- *Even if the scientists had found out about uranium 235 much sooner, the bomb could not have been made until the 1930s or 40's. Why not?*

- *Einstein had suggested that the new energy might be used to generate power, but the Manhattan Project was concerned only with his second suggestion – a bomb. Why?*

Source 134 Hiroshima after the explosion, 1945

THE MANHATTAN PROJECT 1942–45

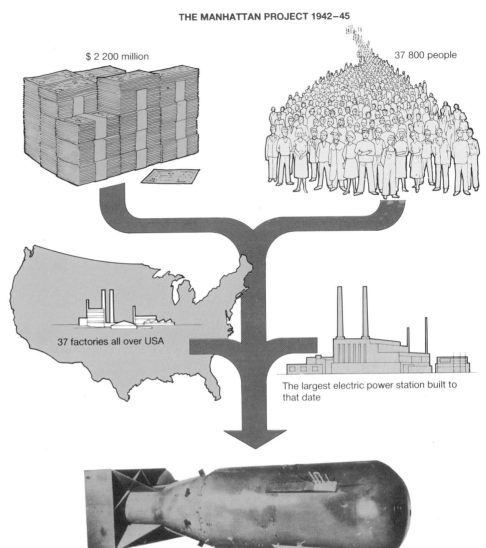

$ 2 200 million

37 800 people

37 factories all over USA

The largest electric power station built to that date

'Little Boy', the bomb that was dropped on Nagasaki

Source 135 Calder Hall, Cumbria, the world's first large nuclear power station, opened October 1956. Its main purpose was to make plutonium for bombs. Small nuclear power plants had operated in the USSR in 1954 and in France in early 1956

Source 136 From the *Guardian*, 4 May 1979

America closes 16 nuclear stations

From our Correspondent in Washington

The United States has been forced to close 16 of its 70 nuclear power stations for safety reasons. Another 14 will probably have to be closed for modifications, and 27 have an acknowledged hazard which is likely to develop unless preventive measures are taken.

Against this background, protest groups are completing plans for a mass demonstration outside the White House and a march on Congress on Sunday to demand a halt to the further development of nuclear plants.

The peaceful use of nuclear power

In making the Atomic Bomb scientists had discovered how to slow down the nuclear reactions so as to control the amount of heat given off. In the 1940s several people saw that this heat could be used to turn water into steam. The steam could then be used in an ordinary turbine to generate electricity.

In the 1950s it seemed possible that Nuclear Power would soon provide an enormous source of very cheap energy.

Source 137 The best thing since fire

However crude and primitive our first nuclear power reactors may appear to future generations, we can look forward with confidence to the time when industrial power from the atom will be a major factor in the world's economy. Indeed it is not too much to say that the exploitation of nuclear energy may come to be regarded as the most important step taken by man in the mastery of nature since the discovery of fire.

Thanks to its pioneer work, this country is well placed to play a leading part in these developments, and because of our strained resources and the rising costs of power from the resources we have been using hitherto, it is particularly important that we should not be left behind in a race

on which our industrial future may depend. (W.S. Churchill, Prime Minister, Speech in House of Commons, 1953)

Source 138 Atomic power will soon take over

The time was coming, Mr. Butler added, when no more coal burning power stations would be built. It might well be that soon after 1965 every new power station would be atomic.
(*The Times* 18 October 1956, R.A. Butler, a Government Minister, at the opening of Calder Hall)

Nuclear power was something completely new. Like other new technologies it ran into difficulties. It was impossible to be sure in advance how much a nuclear power station would cost or how long it would take to build. So many cost more than had been expected and took longer to build.

Opposition to nuclear power

1 Some people have opposed nuclear energy, because some reactors can be used to produce plutonium from which nuclear weapons can be made. So governments keep nuclear power stations under careful control.

Source 139 Cartoon from a French newspaper, 1979

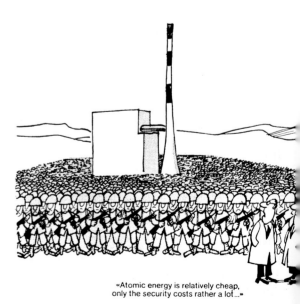

«Atomic energy is relatively cheap, only the security costs rather a lot...»

2 There have been serious fears about safety. These fears increased after an accident at an American Nuclear Power Station at Three Mile Island, Pennsylvania, in April 1979. The trouble was brought under control and nobody was killed or injured.

■ *If nobody was hurt in the Three Mile Island accident, why were people so frightened?*

3 Others have argued that there was no need for this new form of energy.

Source 140 Plenty of fossil fuels
We should by 1980 be able to produce enough . . . coal . . . oil . . . gas and hydro-electricity to meet the energy demand.

This . . . completely eliminates the need for any nuclear energy whatsoever and I am firmly of the view that consideration should be given to ending the nuclear programme and phasing the present stations out.
(Arthur Scargill, President of the Yorkshire Miners. 1978. From his evidence against a plan to extend the nuclear plant at Windscale, Cumbria)

■ *Why should a miners' leader put forward this argument?*

4 Another reason for opposition has been the fear of nuclear pollution (See page 83)

The growth of nuclear power
Nuclear power has not grown as fast as people thought it would in the 1950s. Some countries, like Australia and Denmark, decided not to build any nuclear power stations. Some of the nuclear stations planned in the USA were cancelled, because businessmen feared that they might not be profitable. Improved coal-burning power stations can produce electricity more cheaply in some areas; it depends on the price of coal.

In spite of these problems, by 1984 there were 327 worldwide nuclear power stations at work. They produced 12 percent of the world's electricity. Another 172 were being built.

■ *Why should France have so many nuclear power stations?*

■ *Have events since 1953 proved that Winston Churchill was right in Source 137?*

■ *Does the history of earlier inventions like the steam engine help you to decide whether Churchill was right?*

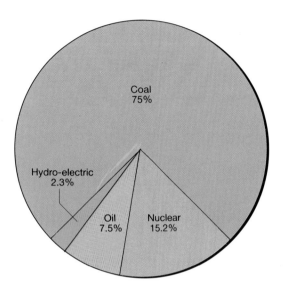

Sources of energy used to generate electricity in Britain, 1983

Table 2 Nuclear power stations in various countries, July 1984

Country	Plants in use	Plants being built	Total
United States	81	47	128
Soviet Union	46	24	70
France	38	23	61
Great Britain	38	4	42
Japan	27	12	39
West Germany	13	9	22
Canada	13	7	20
Spain	6	8	14
Sweden	10	2	12
India	6	5	11
South Korea	3	6	9
Czechoslovakia	6	2	8
Belgium	5	2	7
Taiwan	4	2	6
Italy	3	3	6
Switzerland	5	—	5
East Germany	5	—	5
Argentina	2	1	3
Brazil	1	1	2
Others	15	14	29
World total	327	172	499

(British Nuclear Fuels Ltd Topical Brief 92)

Energy and everyday life

Source 141 Yorkshire miners at work, about 1900

■ How much of the miners' work would have been done in the same way 300 years earlier?
■ What new machines and types of energy would be used for this work today?

Steam power was used mainly on the railways and in factories. A few steam engines were used on farms and for road transport and there were also some big steam cranes and shovels. But until well into the twentieth century, the work done away from the factory and the railway line was done by horses and by human muscles, not by machines.

Source 142 Electrically-driven machines in a Manchester engineering works during the First World War

Source 143 Hard work on the farm

When I was ten I left school to work on a farm for £3 a year and my keep; later I got £5. As a carter's lad I helped to drive the horses, and when there were two I had to walk between them and often got trodden on.

On Sundays I walked ten miles home to have dinner with my parents, and then walked ten miles back to start milking.

When not ploughing I carried coal from the pits. Coal was 3d a hundredweight (1.25p for 50 kilos), and they would throw in an extra hundredweight or so for good measure.

It took a team of three horses to carry a load of thirty hundredweight and you'd be at it from six in the morning until nine at night. One winter's day my team fell down on the ice coming from Biddulph, and I had to remove their shoes and take them to a smith to be sharpened before I could get my load back to the farm. There was little farm machinery used in those days. 'Hand work is best work' my master used to say, and he did not like to have even a horse in the field. Corn was cut with a short hook and hay was cut with a scythe. (At one time Tom worked as a labourer, breaking stone with a sledgehammer.) Rates of pay were 6d (2.5p) a ton for large stone. A man could break a ton a day if he worked hard.
(Tom Mullins, farmer. Born 1863. Memories recorded 1941. From J. Burnett: *Useful Toil*, 1974)

■ *How much of Tom Mullins' work would have been done in the same way a thousand years earlier – or two thousand?*

■ *How much of his work would have been done in the same way sixty years later? What new machines and types of energy would be used for this work today?*

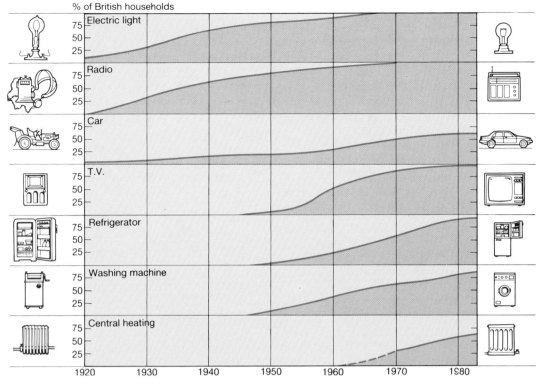

% of British households

Electric light — 75, 50, 25

Radio — 75, 50, 25

Car — 75, 50, 25

T.V. — 75, 50, 25

Refrigerator — 75, 50, 25

Washing machine — 75, 50, 25

Central heating — 75, 50, 25

1920 1930 1940 1950 1960 1970 1980

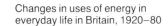
Changes in uses of energy in everyday life in Britain, 1920–80

Source 144 Domestic work in the 1920s

Kitchen maid's duties – rise at five-thirty, clean the flues, light the fire, blacklead the grate, clean the shoes.

The first morning I cleaned them, Mary, the under-housemaid said, 'You haven't done the bootlaces! Don't you know you have to iron the bootlaces? Take them all out and iron them.' So I had to take the laces out of the shoes and iron them. Of course there were no electric irons, just flat irons. They had to be heated in front of the fire and that took nearly a quarter of an hour.

The worst job was when they had minced beef cake. The raw beef, generally a fillet, had to go through a mincer. This wasn't easy. But then I had to get it through a wire sieve, still raw, so you can imagine how long this took. I thought it was impossible when I first tried.

(Staying with a friend) I once went to stay with Olive. The village was three miles from the nearest bus stop, so that meant over an hour's walk with my luggage. There was no water laid on, no electricity or gas, just oil lamps at night. You got water from a well in the garden. Everything tasted of smoke – her mother only had an open fire to cook on.

(Margaret Powell: *Below Stairs* 1968. Margaret was born in 1910. She worked as a domestic servant from the age of 15)

- *What effect had the high energy developments of the twentieth century had:*
  a) *on Margaret's work;*
  b) *on the lives of Olive's family?*

The graphs above give the figures for Britain. In the USA many of these changes began up to twenty years sooner than in Britain.

- *Which fuels were used to provide the energy for these machines?*

- *From the information in these graphs, when would you expect the demand for energy to increase most rapidly?*

People became dependent on high energy supplies. Once people came to rely upon a regular supply of a large amount of energy there were great difficulties when it was cut off. The power cut in Source 145 affected 30 million people. It lasted 14 hours.

- *Has high energy use become as essential to us as fire was to the people of the Stone Age?*

Source 145 From *The Times*, 10 November 1965

Power failure blacks out New York

25,000 stranded in subway traffic chaos at rush hour

From our own Correspondent, Washington, Nov. 9

A massive power failure plunged New York City and parts of New England in darkness tonight. Boston, up-state New York, most of Connecticut, Toronto and Montreal in Canada were affected. The black out occurred at 5.30 this evening at the height of the New York rush hour. Underground trains and lifts in the city's skyscrapers came to a standstill. Hospitals were served by emergency generators. The black out was caused by a break at the switching station on the Niagara power system. Some power was restored by 10 p.m. About 250,000 people were stranded in the Underground. Pandemonium broke out in subway stations, with thousands of city workers caught on station platforms, or in trains whose doors could not be opened.

Police emergency squads were rushed to a prison near Boston tonight when mass rioting broke out soon after the black out.

Patterns of change

A great increase in energy use

The increase in energy use shown in the graph is enormous. More fossil fuel was used in the 29 years from 1950 to 1979 than in the whole of human history before 1950. Why has this happened?

Reasons for the increase

1 One reason is shown on the graph. The world's population has risen. These extra people need extra energy. But the world's population has risen much faster in the countries with few energy resources than in the energy-rich countries. So the rise in population is only part of the explanation for the increase in energy use.

2 Another reason is that more countries have become high energy users. In 1875 there were only four such countries. In 1979 there were 52.

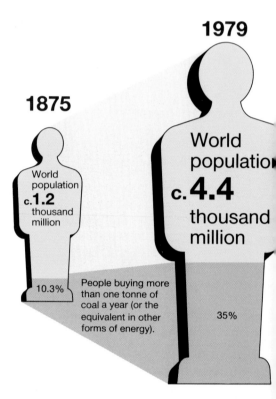

1875

World population **c.1.2** thousand million

10.3%

1979

World population **c.4.4** thousand million

People buying more than one tonne of coal a year (or the equivalent in other forms of energy).

35%

The city of Tokyo by night

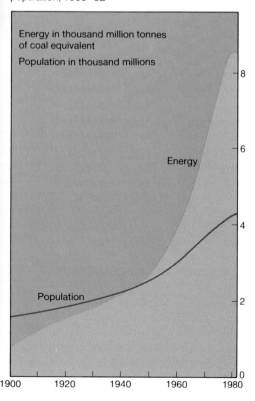

Changing world energy demand and world population, 1900–82

Energy in thousand million tonnes of coal equivalent

Population in thousand millions

Energy

Population

1900   1920   1940   1960   1980

3 The main reason for the great increase in energy used is that the 'high energy countries, new and old, have used more and more. Many new machines have come into use since 1950 in our homes and for transport. Much of the extra energy used in the rich countries is also used in industry. In factories more and more automatic machines have taken over from human labour. Some quite new industries, like the making of plastics, use very large amounts of energy. On farms, oil-burning combine harvesters and green-houses have come into use.

Changes in the sort of energy used
Look at the graph on the right.

- *Why has the use of oil increased more rapidly than the use of the other energy sources?*

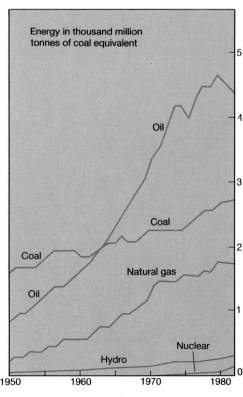

Energy in thousand million tonnes of coal equivalent

Oil

Coal

Coal

Natural gas

Oil

Nuclear

Hydro

1950   1960   1970   1980

Changing sources of world energy, 1950–82

Problems of high energy civilisation

1 A shortage of energy?

By 1970 so much energy was being used that people began to worry about the possibility of a world shortage.

The increase was mostly in the use of the fossil fuels, especially oil and natural gas. How long will the earth's reserves last? The problem is not urgent for coal, but oil and natural gas are being used much faster than new reserves are being discovered.

■ *How long would the reserves of oil known to exist in 1982 last, if we carried on using it at the same rate?*

■ *How long would the reserves of natural gas known to exist in 1982 last if we carried on using it at the same rate?*

More reserves are being found, but the earth is only of fixed size, and much of it has been carefully explored already. So it is not likely that the geologists can go on finding extra supplies for ever. And as oil has to be brought from more and more awkward places, like the Arctic or the sea-bed, it is bound to cost more.

Since about 1970 people and governments in many countries have begun to talk about the 'Energy Problem' and to make plans to meet it.

Source 146 **A problem for Britain**
Our standards of living and well-being depend on adequate supplies of energy. So, too, do the hopes of the developing world. We have become accustomed to oil and natural gas being available in plenty to power the world's economic growth. The future is very uncertain, but there is now wide agreement that world oil supplies cannot continue to increase for much more than a decade or two and will thereafter become increasingly scarce and expensive. This poses a serious problem. The world as a whole will need to turn to other sources of energy, and so, despite our present relative affluence in energy, will the UK.
(British Government Discussion Paper, 1978)

■ *What 'other sources of energy' might the world turn to?*

■ *As well as finding new sources of extra energy what other ways are there for tackling the problem?*

Oil

Underground reserves proved to exist in 1982 92 thousand million tonnes

Amount used in 1982 2.8 thousand million tonnes

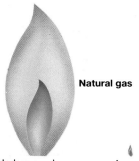

Natural gas

Underground reserves proved to exist in 1982 3 million million cubic metres

Amount used in 1982 0.06 million million cubic metres

World oil and gas used, and known reserves, 1982

Britain in AD 2025?

2 Pollution

Source 147 China's smog

China's industrial pollution is so bad that many cities are now under a pall of heavy smog for 200 days of a year, a top Chinese environmentalist said yesterday in the China Daily.
(*The Guardian*, 12 November 1983)

Oil pollution

An accident to a large tanker can spill hundreds of thousands of tons of oil into the sea. This can kill sea birds and fish, and if it washes ashore it can foul miles of beaches and rocks. Smaller accidents and mistakes while unloading do less damage, but are much more common.

Coal pollution

In industrial towns in the nineteenth and early twentieth centuries coal smoke caused thick fogs. It blackened buildings and helped to cause many diseases. Since the 1950s smoke control laws in many countries have forced people to use fireplaces and furnaces which do not cause black smoke. But the fumes from burning coal still contain many harmful chemicals which can be carried high in the air. They then fall to earth again as acid rain which damages trees and wildlife.

Nuclear pollution

There is a special pollution problem caused by nuclear energy. The waste materials are radioactive. This means that they give off invisible but poisonous radiation, which can be fatal in high doses. So they have to be handled very carefully.

About 1 percent of the waste is highly radioactive and is likely to remain dangerous for at least 1000 years. It is stored in special containers. The engineers of the nuclear industry say that these are quite safe. One problem is to reassure people that they will stay safe for over 1000 years.

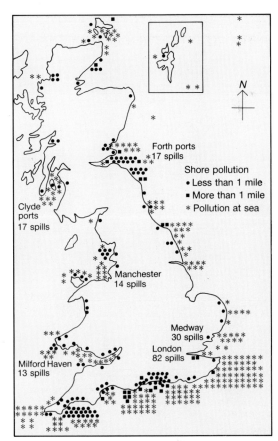

Forth ports
17 spills

Shore pollution
• Less than 1 mile
■ More than 1 mile
* Pollution at sea

Clyde ports
17 spills

Manchester
14 spills

Medway
30 spills

London
82 spills

Milford Haven
13 spills

N

Most of the waste material is not very radioactive, and it has been either buried or dumped in the sea. As with the highly radioactive material, the nuclear engineers say that this is quite safe. Some other people are not so confident.

Source 148 Nuclear waste dumped at sea

Japan and Britain are to dump radioactive waste at sea.

An agreement not to do so for two years was made at the London Convention on Ocean Waste Dumping in February. The convention voted 19 to 6 for a non-binding resolution proposed by Spain: Japan, Britain, the US, the Netherlands, Switzerland and South Africa voted against.

Officials from the Japanese Natural Resources and Energy Agency announced that Japan would ignore the agreement. Japan has 24 nuclear power stations in operation; another 30 are due to start up by 1990. But the rapidly growing industry has been called 'a mansion without toilets' by critics because of the problems of waste disposal. (*The Guardian*, 1 March 1983)

Source 149 From the *Guardian*, 24 May 1978

■ *Are there any sources of energy which have no pollution problems?*
■ *How do the pollution problems of the high energy world differ from those of earlier periods?*

Source 150 From the *Sunday Times*, 19 August 1984

Black snow blamed on power stations

Coal-burning power stations in the Midlands and north of England are being blamed for a heavy fall of foul-smelling highly-acid black snow in the Cairngorms last winter.

The black snow fell early in the morning of February 20 and covered an area of about 75 square miles of the High Cairngorms. 'We had seen nothing like it in the whole of our five years of working in the Cairngorms,' Dr Liz Morris, of the Institute of Hydrology, said. 'It left a black stratum about six inches deep in the snow pack.' For weeks after, every time we dug into the snow we came across this black layer.'

The scientists and their leader, Trevor Davies, are reluctant to discuss their findings before publication in the scientific journals, but The Sunday Times has discovered that they lay most of the blame on the clusters of coal-burning power stations in the Trent Valley and South Yorkshire run by the Central Electricity Generating Board.

The board says that while it does have nine coal-burning stations in the Trent Valley and four in South Yorkshire, it can make no comment on the black snow.

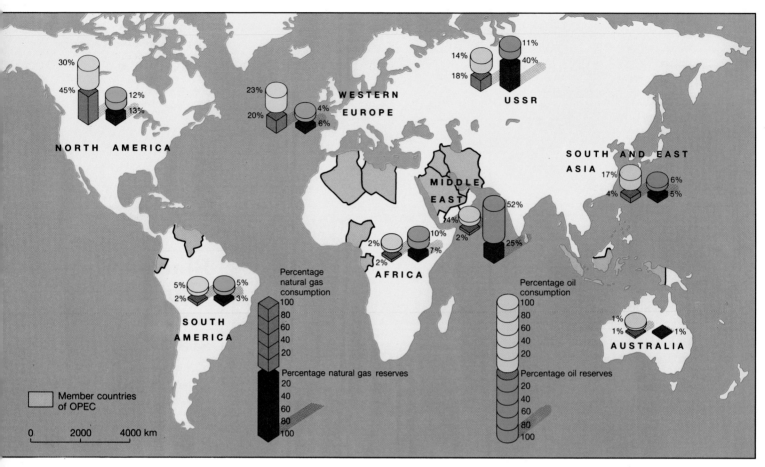

Percentage natural gas consumption
100
80
60
40
20

Percentage natural gas reserves
20
40
60
80
100

Percentage oil consumption
100
80
60
40
20

Percentage oil reserves
20
40
60
80
100

Member countries of OPEC

0   2000   4000 km

Producers and consumers of oil and natural gas, 1982

3 World politics: energy producers v. energy users

World trade in oil brought new difficulties and dangers. When every country controlled its own supplies of wood or coal or water-power, there was no danger of an enemy or a rival cutting the supply line. But in 1982 many countries that used large amounts of gas and oil had to buy it from overseas.

The main energy users were the industrialised countries of Europe and North America. They had developed the oil business. They had the capital needed to search for oil, to drill wells, make pipe lines, and build supertankers. They had the steel and the skilled geologists and the engineers. They had the markets for the oil and the gas.

The main energy producers were in the less developed parts of the world, especially in the Middle East.

The governments and people of these oil producing countries did not like

their oil business being controlled by foreign oil companies. These were mainly American or European and their main aim was to make a profit for their shareholders. In 1960 a group of oil producing countries formed the 'Organisation of Oil Exporting Countries' (OPEC). They felt that if they all worked together they could drive a much better bargain with the rich oil companies.

Until 1973 OPEC was not very successful. But in that year a war broke out between Israel and some of her Arab neighbours. The Arab countries which were members of OPEC immediately stopped supplying oil to countries that supported Israel. So oil became scarce and prices rose rapidly.

Five years later, in 1978, there was a revolution in Iran, which cut off Iranian oil for a time. Once more there was a scarcity and the price rose. Everybody knew that a world shortage of oil and gas was coming within a few years, so OPEC was able to keep up the higher prices. In 1973 the price of crude oil was about $3 a barrel. By 1980 it was $30.

These increases in price caused the price of petrol and other oil products to rise rapidly all over the world. This in turn put up the price of everything else, and helped to cause a recession. Firms closed down. Millions of people became unemployed. The sudden rise in the cost of energy was only one of the causes of this, but it was an important one.

- *What might the governments of the rich oil-using countries do to prevent this sort of thing happening again?*

- *What would be the effect of the increase in oil prices on poor countries?*

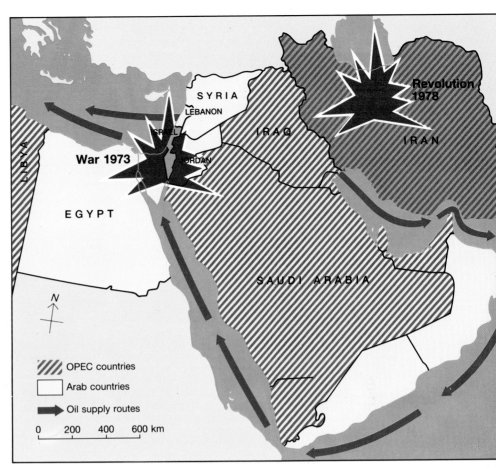

Middle East crises in the 1970s

The effects of a rise in the price of oil. The photograph above was taken in the USA in 1979

4 The low energy world

Nearly two thirds of the people on earth still live a low energy way of life. The people in the village in the pictures on the right and in many thousands of similar ones, rely on forms of energy which they do not need to buy. They find fuel and grow animal fodder near their own village, just as their ancestors have done for four thousand years. In spite of this they are faced with as serious an energy problem as the people in the high energy countries.

This is partly because the population is rising rapidly. There were 600 million Indians in 1975, but by the year 2000 there will be about 1000 million. Already there are so many people in some villages that fuel must be carried long distances.

Source 151 Cooking in the village of Akbarpur, India, 1978. Most of the energy used in villages like this is used for cooking. The main fuels are wood, animal dung or straw

1.5 thousand million people in high-energy countries

1.8 thousand million people in low-energy countries

1 thousand million people in lowest-energy countries

Who buys the world's energy supplies? This diagram deals with energy which is bought and sold

Source 152 Women carry wood eight kilometres

In the last twenty or thirty years the forests of many villages have disappeared. Women now have to walk eight to ten kilometres to meet their fuelwood needs. They have to walk with a heavy load of wood and grass on their backs over rocks and mountains. Sometimes they fall and lose their lives. They have to get up at 4 a.m. and cover long distances on an empty stomach. Some of their songs express their resentment. One of the considerations for parents at the time of their daughter's marriage is to select a groom from a village near to the forest.
(C.P. Bhatt and S.S. Kunwar: *Hill Women – Their Involvement in Forestry*, Chamoli India, 1978)

Similar changes have happened in other parts of India and also in Africa and South America. At the same time forests have been cleared for other reasons as well as to provide fuel. So the world faces a shortage of firewood just as it faces a shortage of fossil fuels.

When the people of Britain faced a shortage of firewood in the sixteenth century, they used coal instead. In India or Africa in the twentieth century the

Source 153 *Top*: Ploughing in Akbarpur, 1978. 90 per cent of the energy used in farming in India or Africa comes from human or animal muscles. *Above*: 20 per cent of the cooking in the village of Akbarpur is done on paraffin stoves

most convenient alternative is paraffin.

If the people of a village want to improve their farming so as to feed the growing number of people, they need oil to run tractors or water pumps.

So when the world price of oil rose so much after 1973, and the rich countries began to worry about a world shortage of energy, people in India and the other poor countries suffered just as heavily.

- *World production of energy would have to more than double to bring the poor countries up to the level of the high energy world. Where could the fuel needed for such a 'levelling up' come from?*

- *Does history suggest that it is likely? What else might happen instead?*

Changes and developments since 1875

In this period many new energy techniques were developed.

1 A new prime mover, the internal combustion engine, was invented.

2 A new way of transmitting energy, electricity, was brought into use.

3 A new form of energy, nuclear energy, was harnessed for human use.

These new techniques enabled machines to take over from muscles at work, in the home, and for transport, making an enormous difference to the lives of everybody in the rich countries.

For this vast amounts of extra fuel were needed, and this need was supplied by oil and natural gas, as well as by coal. A world trade in these fossil fuels sprang up. In recent years fear of a world shortage has led to price increases and many other problems.

By the 1980s the high energy way of life had spread outside Europe. It is now enjoyed by about a third of the world's population.

The poorest of the world's population still rely on muscle power and on wood for fuel. But the supply of fuel wood is running short at a time when oil and gas are becoming too dear for them to buy. So the energy problem is much more serious for them than for anybody else.

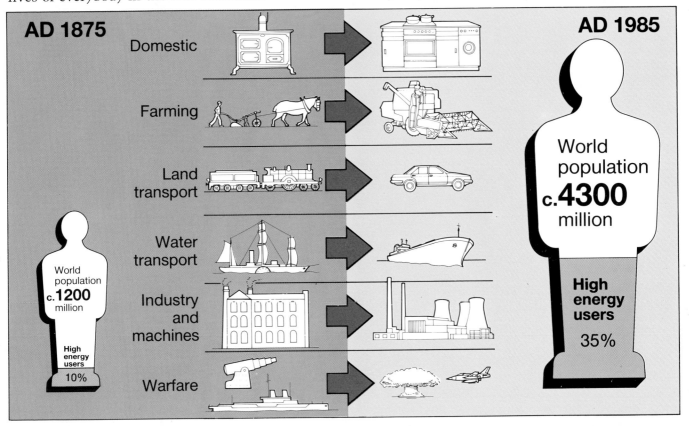

AD 1875 · AD 1985

Domestic

Farming

Land transport

Water transport

Industry and machines

Warfare

World population c.1200 million — High energy users 10%

World population c.4300 million — High energy users 35%

Postscript

A good story should have a beginning, a middle and an end. History is not so neat and tidy.

Human beings tamed fire and used it as part of their hunting way of life. They used simple energy techniques like animal power and water power to build up civilisations and to spread them across the globe. The complex energy techniques of the last 200 years brought about a much more powerful and richer civilisation in some parts of the world.

Will this rich and powerful civilisation spread to the rest of the world? Will new techniques provide further massive increases of energy supply? Will more efficient or less extravagant ways of using energy enable high energy civilisation to live within its income?

For the answers to these interesting and important questions we must wait until the twenty-first century.

SOME FACTORS IN THE HISTORY OF ENERGY

Some things keep coming up again and again in history. For instance people have fought wars at every period, and wars have often affected the history of energy. Another theme that keeps coming back again and again is transport. From the prehistoric farmer carrying a bundle of firewood, to the modern super-tanker carrying oil, transport has been important in the history of energy. These long-lasting themes are called 'factors'.

This book discusses five factors: Transport, War, Shortage, Government and Ideas. How many factors really matter? Just these five? Or could other factors have been chosen?

Looking at each factor in turn is easier than looking at several at once, but it can be misleading. In history dozens of different factors work together, some pulling in one direction, some in others. So no one factor can by itself 'cause' something to happen. For instance war played an important part in the coming of nuclear power, but so did science, so did industry and so did governments. Looking at factors one by one is a useful way of studying the history of energy in detail. But to explain why things happened when they did, historians need to explain how many factors worked together over a period of time.

6 War and energy

In all periods of history there has been conflict and war, and the people with the most powerful weapons have usually won.

This section deals with three important developments in the history of energy: horses, gunpowder and nuclear energy. Each of them has peaceful as well as warlike uses, so perhaps they would have happened in any case, even without their use for war.

In each of the three developments, horses, gunpowder and nuclear energy, you should ask the same question.

■ *Did war just speed up changes that were happening in any case or did it start new ones?*

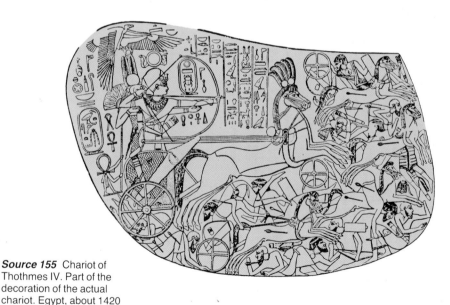

Source 154 Four-wheeled chariots, from a mosaic from Ur, Mesopotamia, about 2600 BC. These chariots are drawn by onagers and controlled by rings in their noses

Source 155 Chariot of Thothmes IV. Part of the decoration of the actual chariot. Egypt, about 1420 BC

Horses

Horse-drawn chariots for war and peace in ancient times

There is little evidence about when or how horses were first tamed. It seems likely that this was done by the nomads of the plains of Western Asia, where wild horses were to be found. But our first clear evidence comes from about 2000 BC, when the Mesopotamians and Egyptians used horses to pull war chariots. Chariots had been used before then, pulled by *onagers*, donkey-like animals slower and weaker than horses. But the speed and power of the horse made the chariot the battle tank of the ancient world. Soon after 2000 BC it was in use in India and in China. For over a thousand years, armies using chariots swept their enemies off the field of battle.

■ *In what ways are these chariots similar to each other? In what ways do they differ?*

■ *What can we tell from this evidence about the importance of chariots?*

Source 156 How chariots were used

In chariot fighting the Britons begin by driving all over the field hurling javelins. Generally the terror inspired by the horses and the noise of the wheels are enough to throw their opponents' ranks into disorder. Then, they jump down from their chariots and fight on foot. In the meantime their charioteers retire a short distance from the battle in such a position that their masters have an easy retreat to their own lines. Thus they combine the mobility of cavalry with the staying power of infantry. By daily practice they attain such skill that even on a steep slope they are able to control the horses at full gallop, and to check and turn them in a moment. They can run along the chariot pole, stand on the yoke, and get back into the chariot as quick as lightning.
(Julius Caesar: *Conquest of Gaul*, written c.52 BC about events in 55 BC.)

This description comes from the very end of the long period when chariots were important weapons, but the British chariots were not very different from the earlier ones.

■ *Is this evidence useful in studying the use of chariots over 1000 years before Caesar's time?*

Source 159 Assyrian hunting chariot. A carving from the palace of Ashur-nasir-pal, Mesopotamia, ninth century BC

Source 160 Greek war-chariot. From a vase of about 500 BC

Source 161 From a Roman carving of Parthian soldiers, about AD 110. The Parthians came from Iran, and their heavily armoured horsemen had defeated the Romans. But like all horsemen in the ancient world they had no stirrups. Horses were very useful for rapid movement, but in battle it was very easy to fall off. The most important troops in a disciplined army like that of the Romans were the foot soldiers.

Riding horses in war and peace in the ancient world

There is no evidence about the first discovery of riding. It may be that nomadic herdsmen tamed wild horses and learned to ride them long before chariots were made. But it is only after about 800 BC that there is evidence of organised cavalry. Cavalry regiments gradually took over from chariots. But though horses could be used, as chariots had been, to move soldiers quickly, not much fighting was done from horseback.

Source 157 Chariots were used for peaceful purposes as well as for war. A Chinese official travelling. A bronze tomb model, second century AD

Source 158 An artist's impression of a British chariot, about 50 BC. It is based on some chariot parts found in a holy pool in Anglesey

Source 162 Norman knights killing Anglo-Saxon foot soldiers. From the Bayeux Tapestry, about AD 1070

Source 163 Nobles out riding. From *Les Très Riches Heures du Duc de Berry*, France, about 1416

Source 164 It took years to learn to wear the heavy armour and to manage the horse in battle. From a manuscript, about 1480

Source 165 Pottery statue from a Chinese tomb, first century BC. Horses like this were a status symbol highly valued by rich Chinese families at the time. They were used for travel, for hunting, or for racing.

Horses for war and peace in the Middle Ages and later

During the European Middle Ages the horse became much more important both for war and for peace than in ancient times. This was made possible by two inventions, the horse collar and stirrups.

From about AD 800 to about AD 1500 mounted knights skilled in fighting on horseback won nearly all the battles. Each knight needed several large and powerful horses. So in Europe heavy horses were bred in large numbers. As well as horses the knight needed a team of half a dozen men to carry and look after his armour and to help him to mount and dismount. It was rather like the crew of a tank in modern war. So the knights came from the class of rich landowners. For over 500 years they dominated every country in Europe. Their power depended on many other things as well as their horses, but their horses were very important. The German word for knight is 'Ritter' or rider. The French word is 'chevalier' or horseman.

During the Middle Ages horses came into widespread use for peaceful purposes as well as for war. By about 1500 AD they had taken over from oxen in parts of Europe, for pulling carts and ploughs.

- *How might the breeding of war-horses have affected this?*

In the years 1500–1800 horses became more and more important as a source of energy. In armies they were needed to move the artillery. The largest type of gun needed 25 horses for the gun itself and another twelve for the powder and shot.

- *How did war influence man's use of the horse?*

- *Did it speed up something that was happening for other reasons, or did it start something new?*

Source 167 Army horses at the siege of a Dutch town, 1606. A contemporary print. In the foreground is a mobile corn mill to feed the army. On the right is the same mill on the move

Source 166 Copper coin issued by a Cumberland colliery, 1797. As the horse turned the large wheel, it lifted coal or water from the mine

Source 168 Above: An advertisement for a twelve-horse engine for driving farm machinery, Wisconsin, USA, 1872. Even after the invention of the steam engine the horse was still the most convenient source of power in many places

Source 169 A cavalry charge at Balaclava 1854. Cavalry formed an important part of all armies until the invention of machine guns and tanks. A painting by R. Caton Woodville in the late nineteenth century

Guns and gunpowder

Source 170 From a Chinese book, AD 1044. This is the earliest description of how to make gunpowder

汉筒长五寸
筒用剖竹为柙长二
尺三寸然有铁镞

Source 171 Chinese rocket-powered arrow. From *Wu-pei-chi*, a Chinese book, 1621

Source 172 An attack on a town. From a French manuscript, 1390

The gunpowder made from the recipe in Source 170 went off with a 'whoosh' rather than a bang, and was used for fire-works as well as for war. By 1120 the Chinese were using bamboo tubes filled with gunpowder in two ways. The first was the 'fire arrow': the tube itself was aimed at the enemy and flew off like a rocket. The second was the 'fire lance': the tube was held on the end of a spear and it spurted flames at the enemy.

By about 1300 some Chinese had thought of making tubes of metal instead of bamboo. But they didn't take the other important step of improving the gunpowder so that it would explode effectively.

It was in Europe that this step was taken. The first real guns were made there about 1320.

Source 173 Guns become common
These instruments which discharge balls of metal with most tremendous noise and flash of fire, were a very few years ago very rare . . . but now they have become as common and familiar as any kind of arms. So quick and clever are the minds of men in learning the most harmful arts.
(Petrarch, Italian poet, writing c.1350)

It is probable that the idea of gunpowder, like so many others at this same period, came to Europe from China.

Once Europeans had made guns they went on to improve them so much that within a few hundred years they had conquered much of the rest of the world, including parts of China. So it was a development of great importance in world history.

Why were guns developed in Europe and not in China?
For most of the time from 1279 to 1644 China was ruled from Peking by a single powerful government. Europe was quite different. It was broken up into many separate countries such as England and France, each with its own government and having its own army and navy.

Source 174 English guns are best
In 1601 Edmund Peake appealed to the House of Commons to forbid the export of cannon. As he pointed out, although the Queen might make £3000 a year out of her custom on exported guns, she lost more than that on cargoes captured or destroyed at sea by enemy ships armed with English guns. He said that the Swedish and Spanish iron founders could not make cast pieces equal in quality to the English. If English guns were withheld, foreigners would be compelled to use the more expensive brass costing £6 for 50 kilos, against 50p. for 50 kilos for cast iron. 'It appears,' he added, 'to be a particular blessing of God given only to England for her defence. For although most countries have their iron, yet none of them all have iron of the toughness to make such iron guns of'. (H.C.Darby: *Historical Geography of England*, 1936)

■ *What does this source suggest about why the Europeans spent so much time and money developing guns?*

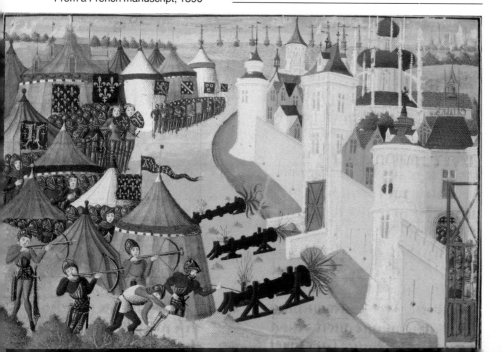

More guns need more metal

As well as helping to make Europe more powerful, the gunpowder and guns were important in another way. These new weapons needed large amounts of metal and many skilled craftsmen.

The diagram shows how the growth of the arms industry in Europe and especially in Britain helped to bring about the industrial revolution.

The making of guns affected the coming of the steam engine in another more direct way. If guns are to shoot straight they must be bored out very accurately. A machine to do this was not invented till 1774. Its inventor, John Wilkinson was a near neighbour and customer of Boulton and Watt, and in 1774 Watt badly needed an accurately bored cylinder for his first steam engine. Wilkinson was able to use his new cannon-boring machine to make one. It is doubtful whether Watt's machine could have been made to work without it.

Peaceful uses of gunpowder

Even gunpowder has its peaceful uses. It is quite probable that it was first used in China for fireworks. This use has gone on ever since.

Of more practical importance is its use for blasting to loosen rock and coal in mines and quarries. This began in the Cornish tin mines about 1700, and as coal mines went deeper it came into common use there too. Without gunpowder the enormous increase in coal output in the eighteenth and nineteenth centuries would have been much more difficult.

- *How did war influence man's use of gunpowder? Did it speed up something that was happening in any case or did it start something new?*

- *What influence did guns and gunpowder have on man's other uses of energy? Did they speed up existing changes or start new ones?*

Guns, gunpowder and the growth of industry in Europe, 1500–1800

Source 175 Sixteenth-century foundry for bronze cannon. From a book published at Antwerp, about 1600. The tread-wheel on the left drives machinery to bore the cannon. Cast iron guns needed an even larger foundry with water-powered bellows and massive supplies of charcoal

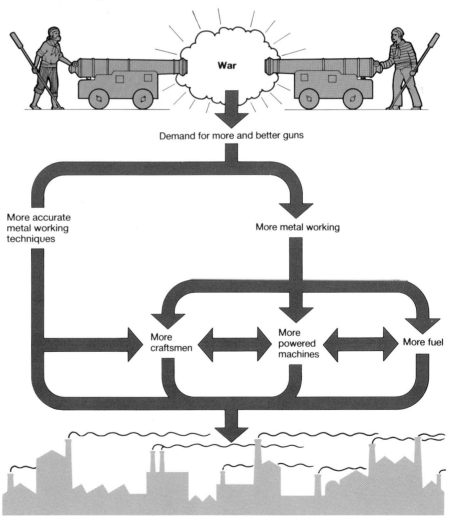

Industrial Revolution in iron, coal and steam

95

War and nuclear energy

There can be no doubt that nuclear energy first came into use as a weapon of war. Look at the account of the events on pages 74–5, and particularly at Einstein's 1939 letter to President Roosevelt (page 74).

- *How did war influence man's use of nuclear energy?*

- *Did war speed up existing changes or start something new?*

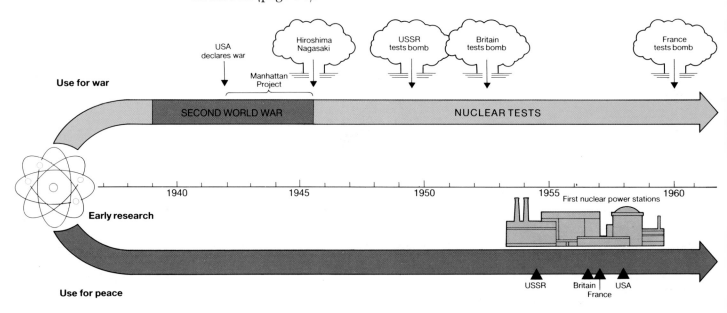

War and energy through time

War influenced the history of energy in many other ways and at many other times.

- *What other examples are there of war playing a part in the history of energy?*

- *Are there examples of war a) starting new energy developments?*

b) *speeding up changes that were happening anyway?* **c)** *slowing down or preventing changes?*

- *Have there been important energy developments that were not affected much by war?*

- *How important has war been in the history of energy?*

7 Transport and energy

Ever since the farmers of the New Stone Age began to live in permanent villages, there has been a fuel transport problem. How was firewood (or other sorts of fuel) to be carried?

This leads to a second question. How far was it worthwhile to go to fetch it? If you have to carry fuel on your own back you will give a different answer to this question than if you have a pack animal or a railway or a super-tanker to carry it for you. With each development in transport the answer to the question 'how far?' has changed.

Transport also affected the history of energy in another way. All transport methods use up energy themselves. The pack-horse has to be fed and looked after. The motor car needs petrol. So when studying how transport has affected the history of energy you should ask:

- *What methods of transport were used at each period?*

- *From how far did people find it worthwhile to fetch fuel?*

- *What sorts of energy were used for transport in each period?*

Source 177 An American Indian farmer carrying wood. A drawing by a Spanish artist, early sixteenth century

Early farming people 8000 BC to 3500 BC

It was with the beginning of farming that the need to transport fuel began, but archaeologists find little evidence of the methods used. Probably the early farmers carried wood on their own backs or on those of their animals. Sources 176 and 177 come from thousands of years later.

- *Would any evidence be left for archaeologists by activities like these?*

- *How far might it be worth going to fetch fuel using each of these methods? (About 10, 25, 50, 100, 500, 1000, or 10000 kilometres?)*

Source 176 A bullock-drawn sled carrying wood. Zimbabwe, twentieth century AD

97

Low energy civilisations, 3500 BC to AD 1500

People living in the early civilisations needed to transport more goods over longer distances than the first farmers had. So it is not surprising that they developed new methods of transport, and improved existing ones. They used four important methods.

For land transport   Pack animals
                               Wheeled carts

For water transport   River boats
                               Sea-going ships

Pack animals

Pack animals could transport goods over long distances, but at high cost.

Source 179   Cost of camel transport

A camel would carry about 500 'libri' (158 kilos). So the cost of goods was doubled by charges along the road. These charges came to something over 10 'denarii' a day for 65 days.
(Pliny: *Natural History*, Rome, first century AD)

Money then and now: An ordinary soldier in the Roman army was paid 100 *denarii* a year.

■ *What did it cost to carry one kilo of goods over this route?*

Source 178 Pack camels in the Gobi Desert, 1920s. This route across Asia was 8000 kilometres long. It was in operation by 200 BC

■ *What was the cost of one kilo at the beginning and end of the journey?*

Here are some figures which compare the cost of carrying goods by various pack animals and by river boat. They were worked out in China in 1929. These are the distances over which the same weight could be carried at the same cost.

Porters	16 km
Pack horses	20 km
Pack donkeys	25 km
Pack mules	34 km
Pack camels	34 km
River boat	133 km

■ *Does the evidence from 1929 tell us anything about transport costs two thousand years earlier?*

Expensive goods like silks or spices could be carried thousands of kilometres by pack animals and still sold at a profit.

■ *What about bulky goods like firewood?*

Wheeled carts

Source 180   Cost of transport by ox wagon, 175 BC

The olive crusher we bought at Suesa (40 km. away) for 400 sesterces and 50 libri (16 kilos) of oil.

To fetch it needed 6 men with 6 boys to drive the oxen for 6 days – 72 sesterces. For setting it up – 60 sesterces.

The complete cost was 629 sesterces.
(Cato 'On Agriculture', Rome, 175 BC. An olive crusher was a machine which included a heavy beam of wood about ten metres long. Olive oil was important for cooking and lighting.)

Money then and now: A *sestercius* would buy two loaves of bread.

- *What speed did the oxen move at? (You must decide first how many hours a day they might spend travelling).*

- *What advantages and drawbacks might wheeled carts have compared with pack animals?*

- *Would it be worthwhile to use wheeled carts to fetch firewood, or charcoal?*

Horses or oxen?

The fastest walking speed of an ox is about 2.4 kph. Horses can walk at about 5 kph, a big advantage. But horses must be fed on grain if they are to work hard and grain is more expensive than the grass and hay eaten by oxen. In the ancient world oxen had another advantage over horses – they could pull four times as much.

Look carefully at the harness of the horses in Sources 182 and 183. The Roman harness tended to throttle the horse. In 1910 a French engineer tested this harness. He found that the horse could pull only 500 kg, about a quarter of the weight it could pull with a modern collar.

The Chinese system, with shafts and a strap round the horse's chest was better than the Roman 'throat strap' type, but still did not let the horse use its full power. So people in ancient times used horses for speed, and oxen for pulling heavy loads.

The padded horse collar is a very simple idea. The padding keeps the collar away from the horse's wind-pipe, so that it can pull about four times as heavy a load as with the old throat strap. After about AD 900 this important invention came into widespread use. A horse with the new harness pulled as much as an ox and pulled it twice as fast. So wheeled transport over land became possible over longer distances, and quicker and more convenient over short ones.

To work hard and steadily, a horse must be fed on oats or barley. The climate of Western Europe is well suited to growing these crops. Also, in the years AD 1000 to 1300 a better system of farming, the 'three field system' came into use in Western Europe. This made it possible for Europeans to grow more oats and barley, and to keep more horses for transport and for other purposes.

The improved horse harness was important and helped to make Europe rich and powerful. But even in Europe, as in the other low energy civilisations transport of goods was much cheaper and easier by water than by land.

Source 181
A Roman ox cart. From a mosaic, about AD 300

Source 182 *Left*: A carving of a Roman horse-drawn wagon. Austria, first or second century AD

Source 183 *Above*: A rubbing of a moulded brick. From about the same time as the Roman wagon. China

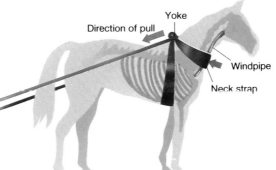

Yoke
Direction of pull
Windpipe
Neck strap

This diagram shows how the yoke harness copied from that used for the ox, tended to choke the horse

Source 184 An Elizabethan street scene, showing the padded horse collar

Source 185 Traffic on the River Tigris at Nineveh, seventh century BC. A wall carving from the king's palace

River boats

Source 186 Boats on the Euphrates

I will next describe the thing which surprised me most of all . . . I mean the boats which ply down the Euphrates to Babylon. These boats are circular in shape and made of hide. They build them in Armenia (about 900 kilometres up the river). They cut willow rods to make the frames and then stretch skins on the underside. They are not tapered at the bow or stern but quite round like a shield. The men fill them with straw, put the cargo on board – mostly wine in palm-wood casks – and let the current take them downstream. They are controlled by two men. The boats vary a great deal in size. Some are very big, the biggest of all having a capacity of fourteen tonnes. Each boat carries a live donkey – the larger ones several – and when they reach Babylon and the cargoes have been offered for sale, the boats are broken up. The frames and straw are sold, and the hides loaded on the donkeys' backs for the return overland to Armenia. (Herodotus: *The Histories*, Greece c. 450 BC)

A modern drawing of a Roman trading ship, second century AD

■ *Is fuel likely to have been carried in boats like these?*

In China, as well as using river boats, they built a network of canals. By AD 500 canals hundreds of miles long linked the Yangtze and the Yellow rivers together. (See map on page 17) The system was so important for the transport of grain from one part of China to another that it was carefully controlled by the government.

The Egyptians were luckier than either the Chinese or the people of Babylon and Nineveh. The wind in Egypt blows from the north nearly all the time, so boats could float downstream with the current and sail upstream against it.

■ *Did rivers give completely free energy for transport?*

■ *From what distance might it be worth-while to fetch fuel by river or canal?*

Sea-going ships

The world map on p.17 shows how far the ships of the early civilisations could travel. They usually only sailed when the wind was right, and not at all in winter if they could help it. They had no compass, and they kept in sight of land as much as possible.

Sea transport was very important to Rome. A special sea port was built at Ostia. From there goods were taken by barge up the river Tiber to Rome. The supply of food and other goods to the city was so important that the Emperor kept it under careful control.

During the Middle Ages the Chinese developed large ships that could cross the Indian Ocean.

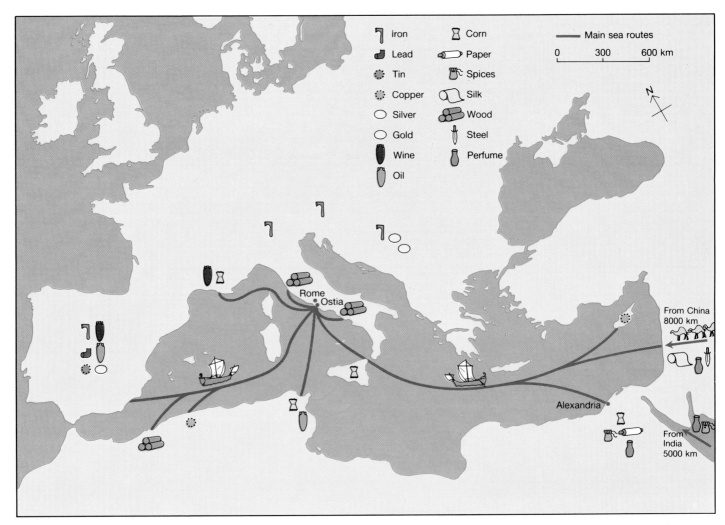

Legend:
- ⌐ Iron
- Lead
- Tin
- Copper
- ○ Silver
- ○ Gold
- Wine
- Oil
- ⌛ Corn
- Paper
- Spices
- Silk
- Wood
- Steel
- Perfume
- —— Main sea routes

0   300   600 km

Rome • Ostia

From China 8000 km

Alexandria

From India 5000 km

Source 187 An Italian describes Chinese ships

We shall first tell about the great ships in which the merchants go and come into India through the Indian sea.

They are mostly built of pine wood. They have one deck and on this deck there are commonly 60 little rooms or cabins. In each a merchant can stay comfortably. They have one good helm which is called a rudder, and four masts and four sails. They often add two masts more, according to the state of the weather. Some ships have as many as 13 holds, that is divisions on the inside. These ships need some of them 300 sailors, some 200, some more some fewer. They carry a much greater burden than ours. They are so large that they carry as many as 5000 baskets of pepper and some 6000.

(*The Book of Marco Polo*, 1299, Italy. Marco Polo travelled in the east from 1275–91.)

Ships with large crews like this were expensive to run, even though they used the free energy of the wind. They were useful only for carrying expensive cargoes like pepper. The Chinese at this time had little need to import goods from across the oceans, but the Europeans did. So it was the Europeans who first made full use of ocean going ships.

■ *In the 'low energy' civilisations before AD 1500, what methods of transport were used?*

■ *What sort of energy did each of these methods use?*

■ *About how far did people find it worth while to transport fuel? (about 10, 25, 50, 100, 500, 100 or 10 000 kilometres?)*

Supplies for the city of Rome, about AD 100

■ *Which of the items imported into Rome were essential and not luxuries?*

101

Transport and the second energy revolution 1500–1875

Source 188 The *Endeavour*: A model in the National Maritime Museum. The *Endeavour* was built at Whitby to carry coal. It was of the same type as the *Diamond* (Source 189)

Ocean-going ships

Captain James Cook sailed round the world and explored New Zealand and Australia in the *Endeavour* in 1769–71. It was about 30 metres long and carried 97 men. Cook's *Endeavour* was much smaller than the Chinese ships of Marco Polo's time, but it was probably more important in world history.

This is partly because the Europeans used ships like it, many of them no bigger, to explore and then conquer many parts of the world in the years 1500–1800. But it is also because Cook's ship was built to carry coal. Cook had learned his job in the coal trade, and he persuaded the navy to buy one of these tough and reliable ships for his great voyage.

Ocean-going sailing ships with large crews could only carry expensive goods like spices, sugar, silver or slaves. But for short distances, ships of the same type but with much smaller crews could carry coal. The transport of large quantities of coal made the 'energy revolution' of the nineteeth century possible.

The second 'energy revolution' would have been impossible without improved transport to carry coal. Most of the goods transported for any distance in the low energy civilisations were light and of high value. But coal was cheap and heavy. So improved transport was essential, overland as well as by sea.

'Sea coal' routes in the eighteenth century

Source 189 The *Diamond* of Scarborough unloading coal on Sandsend beach, 1889. The *Diamond* was very like the ships which had been used in the coal trade for a hundred years before Captain Cook's time

Source 190 How coal was transported in 1724

The coals are dug in a pit a vast depth in the ground, sometimes fifty, sixty to a hundred fathoms (185 metres), and being loaded into a great basket or tub, are drawn up by a wheel and horse or horses to the top of the shaft. There they are thrown out upon the great heap, to lie ready until the ships come into the port to demand them. They are then loaded again into a great machine, called a waggon, which by means of an artificial road, called a waggon-way, goes with the help of but one horse, and carries two cauldron (2.6 tonnes) and more at a time. This goes sometimes three or four miles to the nearest river. There they are . . . thrown into a great store-house, called a Stethe, made with one part hanging over the water, so that the lighters or keels can come close under it. The coals are at once shot into the said lighters, which carry them to the Ships. This I call the first loading upon the water. From the lighters they are thrown by hand into the ships, which is the second loading.

From the ships, being brought to London, they are delivered into coal lighters in the river, which is the third loading.

From those lighters into the great west country barges, perhaps for Oxford or Abingdon, which is the fourth loading.

From these barges they are loaded into carts and waggons to be carried to the country town to the last consumer, which is the fifth loading.
(Daniel Defoe: *Tour through the Whole Island of Great Britain* 1724–7)

■ *What means of transport are mentioned by Defoe?*

■ *What sources of energy do they use?*

■ *About how far was coal being transported?*

Source 191 High cost of carrying coal
The Borough of Abingdon is very populous and depends only on trade and is situated where fuel is very dear, and therefore the inhabitants are chiefly obliged to make use of coals which they purchase at a very great price, by being brought from London by water, that is about 80 miles (130 kilometres) and are obliged to pay 18 shillings (90p.) for the carriage of every cauldron (1.3 tonnes) of coal.
(Petition of the mayor and citizens of Abingdon to the House of Commons, 3 April 1738. Commons Journals.)

■ *The distance from London to Abingdon by road is only about 58 miles. Why didn't they take the coal by road?*

Source 192 The wagon is running on the 'artificial road' (made of wood) and the 'stethes' and lighter (river boat) is in the background. The wagon is running downhill controlled by a brake. From J. Morand, *The Art of coal mining*, France, 1768

Source 194 Ten miles is too far

A coal mine may exist in the United States not more than 10 miles from very valuable ores of iron and other materials and both be useless as the price of land carriage is too great to be borne by either.
(U.S. Senate Committee 1816)

■ *What might the US Senator go on to suggest?*

Source 195 The Bridgewater Canal

At its upper extremity in Worsley (the canal) buries itself in a hill. It enters by an arch wide enough for the admission of long flat-bottomed boats which are towed by means of hand rails on each side. This passage penetrates for near three-quarters of a mile before it reaches the first coal works. The boats hold seven or eight tons, and several of them being linked together. They are sent along the canal to Manchester (17km) in strings drawn by a horse or two mules.

By the Act of Parliament for making this canal, the Duke was limited to a rate not exceeding two and sixpence (22.5p.) per tonne, and was bound to sell his coals at Manchester and Salford for no more than 4d. per hundred. (1.5p. for 50kg) The poor of those towns were benefited by a reduction in the price of coals of one half of what they before paid, and vast quantities were taken by them from the wharf in Castlefield in wheel barrows at 3.5d a hundred (1.4p for 50kg).
(J. Aikin: *Description of the country round Manchester*, 1795)

Loads for one horse c.1800

Pack horse	127 kilograms
Pulling wagon	
on soft road	637 kilograms
on hard road	2.04 tonnes
on iron road	8.16 tonnes
Pulling barge	
on river	30.6 tonnes
on canal	51 tonnes

(*Oxford History of Technology*, 1957, based on contemporary figures from engineers of the eighteenth century)

■ *How do you think the coal was transported to Manchester before the Bridgewater Canal was built?*

■ *Why were many canals and horse-drawn railways built in Britain in the years 1760–1800?*

■ *How would this affect the price of coal and the amount of coal produced?*

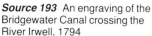
Source 193 An engraving of the Bridgewater Canal crossing the River Irwell, 1794

Steam takes over

Improved ways of using old methods of transport like the horse or the sailing ship helped to start the second 'energy revolution'. In the nineteenth century, steam engines made possible completely new methods of transport: the railways and steamships. This meant that far more coal could be produced.

In 1800 British canals, ships and horse-drawn railways were able to carry over 11 million tonnes of coal away from the mines. In 1913, using steam railways and steam ships, over 25 times as much was carried. Britain's high energy way of life would have been impossible without this. In 1913 some of this coal was still carried by canal or by sailing ship, but most of it was moved by steam transport.

How far was it worth carrying coal?

It is easy to answer this question for the coal that was used in steam ships and railway engines. No other fuel was as good. By 1900 the Trans-Siberian Railway was completed across Asia, and other long railways in America and Africa.

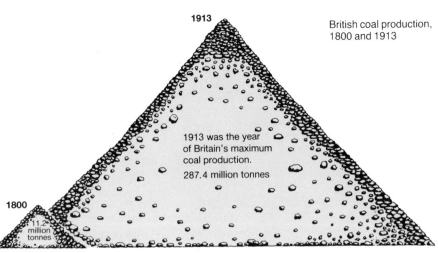

British coal production, 1800 and 1913

1913

1913 was the year of Britain's maximum coal production.

287.4 million tonnes

1800

11.2 million tonnes

Source 196 The scene on 10 May 1869 when the first railway across the American continent was finished. The men on the right had built the line from the east. There was no wood on the plains, so their locomotive has a tall chimney and burned coal. The men on the left had built the line from the Pacific coast. There was no coal in California but plenty of wood, so their locomotive was a wood burner. A tonne of coal has over three times as much energy as a tonne of wood. So wood-burning locomotives were only used in forest areas

World railways and shipping routes, about 1900

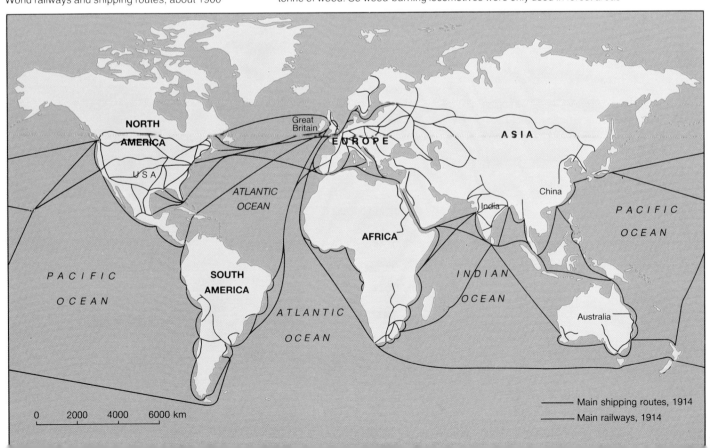

NORTH AMERICA

Great Britain

EUROPE

ASIA

USA

ATLANTIC OCEAN

China

India

PACIFIC OCEAN

AFRICA

SOUTH AMERICA

INDIAN OCEAN

PACIFIC OCEAN

ATLANTIC OCEAN

Australia

0   2000   4000   6000 km

———— Main shipping routes, 1914
———— Main railways, 1914

Source 197 This four horse-power machine was made in Italy but tested in England in 1850

■ Why should people go on with the idea of the horse-powered railway even after the coming of the steam locomotive?

The transport of coal for other purposes, however, was still expensive and the further the coal was taken away from the mines, the more it cost. This is why the first industrial towns had grown up near the coalfields of Britain. The same happened in other European countries and in the USA as these countries became industrialised. So even in 1900 most coal was not carried very far. Britain was the only country that exported very much of it.

Use the map of Britain and the information about exports to decide how far most British coal was being carried about the year 1900.

■ *What difference had steam transport made to the distance British coal was carried?*

■ *What new methods of transport were used between 1500 and 1875?*

■ *What sources of energy did they use?*

■ *About how far could fuel be transported?*

Where British coal was used in 1900

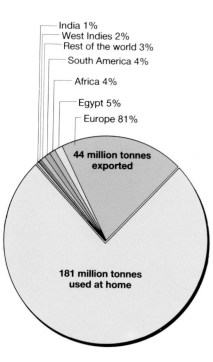

- India 1%
- West Indies 2%
- Rest of the world 3%
- South America 4%
- Africa 4%
- Egypt 5%
- Europe 81%

44 million tonnes exported

181 million tonnes used at home

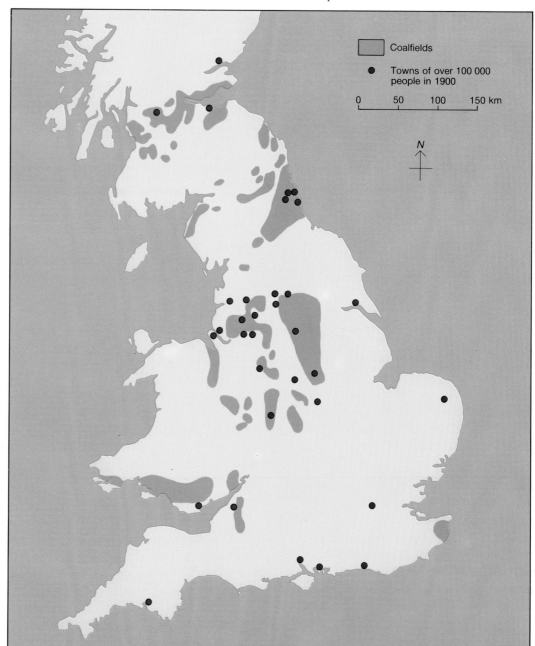

Coalfields

● Towns of over 100 000 people in 1900

0   50   100   150 km

N

Transport and energy in the twentieth century

World oil movements by sea, from BP Energy Review, 1982

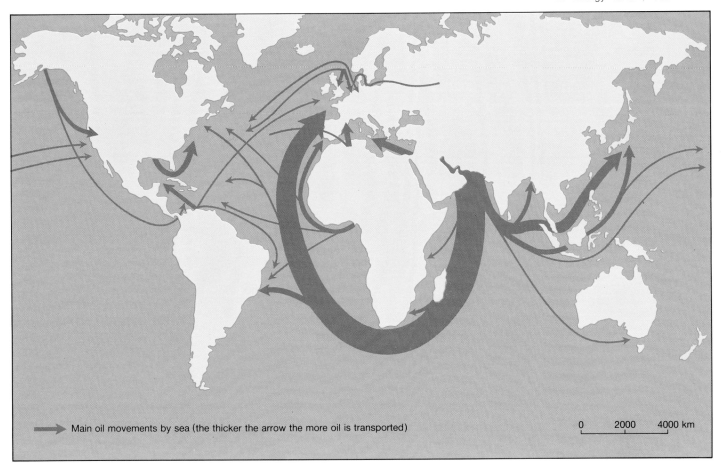

Main oil movements by sea (the thicker the arrow the more oil is transported)

0   2000   4000 km

Transport uses more energy

Since 1900 the people of the 'high energy' countries have greatly increased the amount of energy they use. (See p.80) They also use more of it on transport. In Britain in 1975 we used for transport 44.8 per cent, or nearly half, of all the energy we used.

- *What new forms of transport have developed since about 1900?*

- *What sort of energy does each use?*

How far can fuel be transported today?

There is a world market in oil. It can be moved from wherever it is produced to wherever it is needed. The same is true of uranium. It is also true of natural gas which can be moved by ship like oil, and for long distances by pipe-line. It is even true of coal. Japan buys coal from the USA, and Britain buys it from Australia.

- *Is it likely that it will ever be worth while to fetch fuels from even greater distances?*

8 Shortage and conservation of energy

At some times and places there has been plenty of fuel. At others there has been a shortage.

■ *What examples can you think of?*

When there was a fuel shortage people usually tried to avoid waste and make best use of scarce supplies. This is what is meant by 'conservation'.

Even when there was really plenty of fuel within easy reach, energy was often expensive. Hard work was needed to chop trees down or to mine for coal, and transport cost time and money. So it made economic sense to use energy carefully even when there was plenty.

When money came into use and fuel began to be bought and sold there were some poor people who could not afford to buy it. So even at times of plenty there have been shortages for some.

The evidence below has been selected to help you to think about the reasons for shortages of energy and about how people tried to conserve it.

■ *What have people done about energy shortages in the past?*

■ *How successful have conservation policies been in the past?*

■ *Is this problem today much the same as it was in other periods of energy shortage, or is it quite different?*

An Amazon Indian family group cooking round a fire, a recent photograph, Brazil

We have very little evidence about fuel problems in the days before writing and civilisation. Most archaeological remains come from areas where there was enough wood to meet the simple needs of nomads.

Prehistoric peoples

Source 198 **No shortage of fuel for modern hunter-gatherers**

A woman gathers in one day enough food to feed her family for three days and spends the rest of her time resting in camp, doing embroidery, or visiting other camps. For each day at home, kitchen routines such as cooking, nut cracking, collecting firewood and fetching water occupy one to three hours of her time. The rhythm of steady work and steady leisure is maintained throughout the year.
(R. Lee and I. de Vore: *Man the Hunter*, Study of the Dobe Bushmen, 1968)

■ *What value has this source as evidence of conditions for hunter-gatherers in the Old Stone Age?*

Low energy civilisations

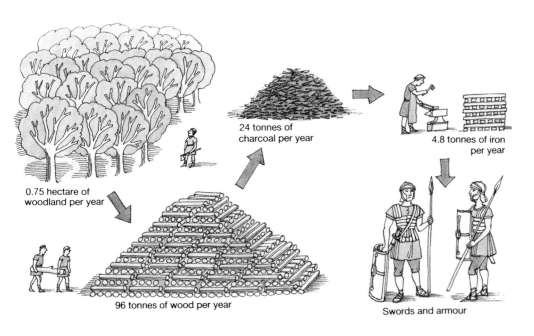

0.75 hectare of woodland per year

24 tonnes of charcoal per year

96 tonnes of wood per year

4.8 tonnes of iron per year

Swords and armour

The amount of wood used by a typical Roman iron furnace

Fuel shortages, 3500 BC to AD 1500

With the coming of metal-working, supplies of fuel were used much more rapidly than before. The figures in the diagram above have been worked out by studying a typical Roman iron furnace. It shows the amount of wood needed to fuel a single furnace for one year.

- *If it took 25 years for the trees to grow again, how big an area would each furnace need over that period?*

Source 199 How Cyprus lost its trees
In ancient times the plains of Cyprus were thickly overgrown with forests and were not cultivated. The mines helped a little against this, since the people would cut down the trees to burn the copper and the silver, and the building of fleets further helped.
(Strabo, *Geography*. Greek, 63 BC–AD 20)

- *Did Strabo agree with cutting down the forests?*

Source 200 Metal working in China
Bellows were violently worked to melt the bronze and the iron: metals flowed forth wastefully for hardening and forging – the work did not cease for a single day. No tall trees were left on the mountain, and the silkworm-oaks and lindera trees disappeared from the groves. Untold amounts of wood were burned to make charcoal. Above, the smoke obscured the very light of heaven and below, the riches of the earth were utterly exhausted
(Huai Nan Tzu: a book written before 122 BC, China)

- *How does this writer's attitude to the removal of the forests compare with Strabo's?*

The cities of the ancient world needed fuel for cooking and heating as well as for industrial uses like metal-working. But they all had good transport systems by river, sea or canal. They could draw on the woodlands of very large areas. So there is not much evidence of a serious shortage, except in some islands.

Ancient woodland like this once covered much of Britain

The Middle Ages

During the Middle Ages, Western Europe had many forests and plenty of rain. These sources of energy were useful when the new West European civilisation began to put itself together out of the broken pieces of the Roman Empire.

Source 201 Plenty of trees

If one walked half a mile, or a mile at most out from the village one came to the edge of the wild, to a wide stretch of moory or boggy ground that formed a temporary barrier and the massed tree-trunks of the primeval forest still awaiting the axe.
(W.C. Hoskins: *The Making of the English Landscape* 1955, describing a typical English village at the time of the Domesday Book, 1086)

In some parts of England, like the New Forest, the ancient woodlands are still there today. But over much of the country the forests were cleared during the 200 years after Domesday Book. This was because the increasing population needed extra land for farming, as well as timber for building and fuel. So by about 1400, poor people in some areas were short of firewood for cooking and heating.

Source 202 Cooking was a luxury

Individual households occasionally and perhaps even frequently bought some of their food cooked, some of their bread baked and some of their ale brewed by others. The reason for this was not only the primitive character of the heating and cooking provision in peasants' houses, but the apparent dearth of fuel . . . By the end of the thirteenth century woodland in most arable areas had been greatly reduced, and burnable timber appeared very dear and presumably scarce; but above all it was owned by the lords. Mediaeval accounts contain frequent references to villagers buying 'underwood' from their lords. On some Glastonbury estates a bundle, apparently quite a small one could be priced at one shilling, or about the price of a bushel (36 litres) of grain. Cooking must have been an expensive operation, something of a luxury and cooked food was not frequently eaten. Porridge and gruel were the commonest family dishes and it is quite possible that some of the porridge was taken as 'brose', i.e. uncooked.
(M.M. Postan: *Mediaeval economy and society*, 1972, writing about conditions in England)

Source 203 There does not seem to be any shortage for this cook! From the Luttrell Psalter, about 1340

Conservation, 3500 BC to 1500 AD

1 Controls on the sale of fuel

Source 204 No dealers allowed
No-one who does not use the public wood scales is to sell charcoal or logs of wood. No-one who has bought any of these products in Delos or aboard a ship in the harbour is to sell any of them. No-one may sell wood, logs or charcoal that is the property of another. No-one except the importer himself is allowed to sell. Importers are not allowed to sell at a higher price than the one they have registered with customs collectors. If anyone makes a sale contrary to the regulations he is liable to a fine of fifty drachmas.
(Laws issued in the Greek island of Delos, 3rd century BC)

Delos today

The fuel situation was most serious in islands like Delos. By this time the trees on Delos had mostly been cut down or destroyed by grazing animals.

2 Burning charcoal instead of wood
Charcoal makes less smoke and fumes indoors than wood, and is more efficient for cooking and heating. It gives off as much heat as about four times its weight in wood, so it is far cheaper to transport. This meant that it paid people to carry fuel from a much greater distance.

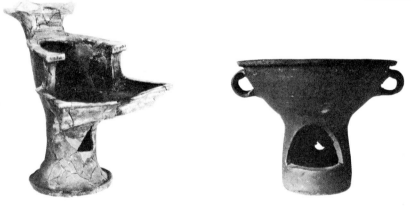

Source 206 *Left*: A charcoal brazier from the second century BC. Found at Delos. *Right*: A modern charcoal brazier bought in Athens in 1976. The drawing below shows how the brazier was used.

Source 205 A Roman iron gridiron over charcoal fire on a brick hearth. Based on museum materials

111

3 Making full use of the sun's heat

Another way of saving fuel was to build so as to take full advantage of the sun. Even in the winter this was worthwhile in the sunny Mediterranean lands.

Source 208 A Roman gentleman describes his country house

This bedroom is very warm in winter when it is bathed in sunshine, and on a cloudy day hot fumes from an adjacent furnace room serve instead. Then you pass through a large and cheerful dressing room, belonging to the bath, to the cooling room, which contains a good sized shady swimming bath. Next to the cooling room is a temperate one which enjoys the sun's kindly warmth, though not as much as the hot room which is built out in a bay. This contains three full plunging baths, two full in the sun and one in the shade.
(Letters of the Younger Pliny, c. AD 100)

Source 207 A reconstructed diagram of the hot room of the public baths at Ostia. Based on archaeological remains

Pliny's house was in the country and he could send his slaves to the forest to cut wood. But 'hypocaust' heating of the type which Pliny used on cloudy days has been estimated to use 128 kilos of wood an hour. This would use up the wood from 10 square metres of land.

- *What arguments might Pliny have used, to explain his careful use of the sun's heat?*

4 Conserving water power

Whatever difficulties there may have been in the supply of wood, the Mediterranean had a much more serious problem with water. In the hot dry summers it could be very scarce. This is probably one of the reasons why the Romans built so few water-mills.

Source 209 Don't waste water: official

a) A fine of five 'libri' of gold shall be inflicted upon those persons who very impudently demand supplies of water that are due to the mills which provide the food supply to the venerable city. Also those persons in charge of the office of prefect of the corn tax shall pay an equal fine if they should consent to the wishes of these most unscrupulous persons.

b) If the greatest houses (have) elegant baths of water we decree that they can have no more than 5cm diameter of water supply pipe. If, by reason of rank, more than this amount is required, by no means shall they have more than 7.35cm each. Houses of inferior merit shall be content with 3cm water pipes. We order that all other persons who maintain houses of smaller size shall have only 1.2cm pipes. Penalty six 'libri' of gold.
(Laws made by the Emperor Theodosius, 22 June, AD 382)

- *What actions did people or governments in Greece and Rome take to deal with energy scarcities?*

- *Which of these were likely to be most effective?*

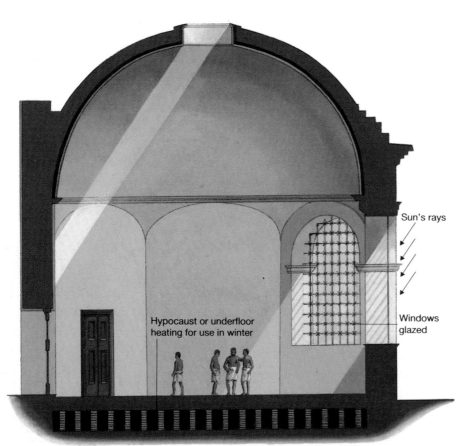

Sun's rays

Windows glazed

Hypocaust or underfloor heating for use in winter

112

Shortage and conservation 1500–1875

Source 210 No need for conservation in Germany

Miners are more likely to exhaust the supply of ores than foresters the supply of wood needed to smelt them. Very great forests are found everywhere, which makes one think that the ages of man would never consume them, especially since nature, so very liberal, produces new ones every day. Besides trees, black stones that occur in many places have the nature of true charcoal . . . (but) . . . the abundance of trees makes it unnecessary to think of that faraway fuel.

(V. Biringuccio: *Pyrotechnia,* Italy, 1540.)

Biringuccio was writing about the important metal producing areas of Austria and Germany.

■ *What were the 'black stones'?*

Source 211 Serious problems in Egypt

Here the problem was everyday cooking, the humble camp fire lit between two stones. Everything was fuel for it: a few sprigs of brushwood, dry plants, straw or esparto grass, the bark of palm trees, 'the dung of camel, horse or ox which is dried in the sun'. Even the privileged cities were not immune from this scarcity. For fuel the people of Cairo used dried dung or the straw from sugar cane, or the very costly wood brought by ships or galleys from Asia Minor to Alexandria. The situation was always precarious. In November 1512 even the officers' kitchen ceased to function for lack of fuel – for who could find fuel near Cairo?

(F. Braudel: *The Mediterranean in the Reign of Philip II,* 1949)

■ *Why was there a problem in Egypt but not in Germany?*

In England the shortage of wood was very serious by the year 1600. This was particularly true in the iron working districts and in the London area.

Source 212 Best trees nearly all gone

He that hath known the weald of Sussex, Surrey and Kent, the grand nursery especially of the oak and beech, shall find such an alteration in less than thirty years as may well strike a fear lest few years more will leave few good trees standing in these wealds.

(John Norden: *The Surveyor's Dialogue,* 1607)

Several ways of dealing with the problem were tried in England.

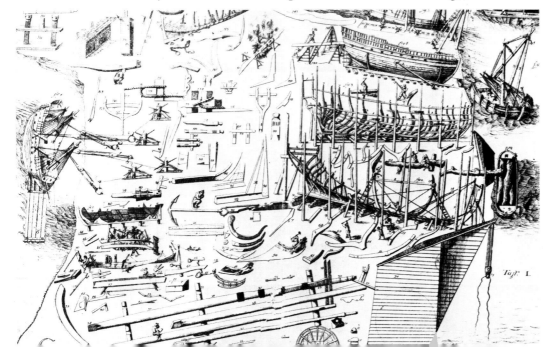

Source 213 A shipyard in Scandinavia, 1692

1 Restrictions on the use of fuel

Source 215 Act of Parliament 1558

To avoid destruction of tymber . . . it is enacted that . . . no person shall convert . . . to charcoal or other fuel for making of Iron any timber tree of Oak Beech or Ash of the breadth of one foot (29cm) square at the stump. This applies to trees growing within 14 miles of the sea or of the rivers Thames, Severn, Wye, Humber, Dee, Tyne, Tees, Trent or any other river by which goods are carried by boat to any part of the sea. This Act shall not apply to the County of Sussex nor to the Weald of Kent.
(Act of Parliament, 1558)

■ *Why did the Act apply only to certain trees?*

2 Replacing sources of fuel

Source 216 How to produce more wood for fuel

It is now in all these parts (West Midlands) usual . . . to enclose land and sow with acorn nuts and ash keys to rear coppice wood. People know by experience that coppice woods are ready money with the iron-masters at any time . . . If the iron works were not in being these coppices would have been . . . turned into pasture and tillage as is done in Sussex and Surrey where the iron works are most of them closed down.
(A. Yarranton: *England's Improvement by Sea and Land,* 1677)

Coppice wood was wood specially planted and cut back every ten years or so to give the maximum supply of wood for fuel.

3 Improved efficiency

One answer to the fuel shortage was the enclosed stove. These used less fuel than open fires and gave out more heat. Stoves built of brick and tiles were common in Germany and Russia in the sixteenth century. From the seventeenth century stoves were often made out of cast iron.

Source 214 A woman in front of the stove. An etching by Rembrandt, Holland, seventeenth century

A drawing of a cooking stove from Munich, Germany. It was designed in 1790 by the scientist Count Rumford. It was carefully insulated and the supplies of air and fuel were carefully controlled, so as to waste little heat. It worked well, but nobody copied the idea until the twentieth century

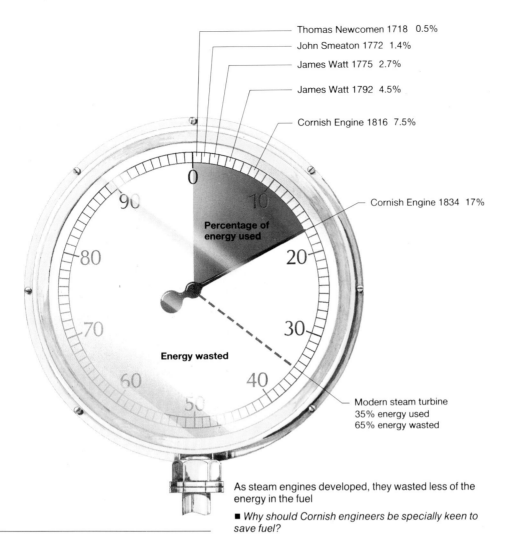

Thomas Newcomen 1718 0.5%
John Smeaton 1772 1.4%
James Watt 1775 2.7%
James Watt 1792 4.5%
Cornish Engine 1816 7.5%
Cornish Engine 1834 17%

Percentage of energy used

Energy wasted

Modern steam turbine
35% energy used
65% energy wasted

As steam engines developed, they wasted less of the energy in the fuel

■ *Why should Cornish engineers be specially keen to save fuel?*

Source 217 An account of the new-invented fireplaces

In these northern colonies the inhabitants keep fires to sit by generally seven months in the year, and in some winters near eight months. Wood, our common fuel, which within these 100 years might be had at every man's door, must now be fetched near 100 miles to some towns and makes a very considerable article in the expense of families. Fuel has become expensive, and as the country is cleared and settled will of course grow scarcer and dearer.

By the help of this saving invention our wood may grow as fast as we can use it, and our posterity may warm themselves at a moderate rate, without being obliged to fetch the fuel across the Atlantic. If pit coal should not be here discovered (which is uncertain) they must necessarily do this. (Benjamin Franklin, Philadelphia USA, 1748. Franklin had just invented a new type of stove.)

4 Using coal instead of wood

The main answer to the shortage of wood and charcoal at this time was to use coal.

In Britain where there was plenty of cheap coal most people could afford to use it wastefully on open fires. But coal for use in steam engines was a different matter. Factory owners looked carefully at the cost of fuel when they decided which steam engine to buy, or whether to stick to water power. The main reason for the success of Watt's engine was that it wasted less coal than the Newcomen engines already in use.

■ *What action did people or governments take in the years 1500–1875, to deal with energy scarcities?*

■ *Were they the same as, or different from those used in earlier periods?*

High energy civilisations

Before 1945: little fear of shortage

Until the nineteenth century, nobody understood how coal or oil had been formed. People thought that they had been placed in the ground by God for our convenience. It seemed likely that more would grow to replace what was used up, in the same way as more crops or trees grew on the surface of the earth.

In this cartoon from *Punch* on 25 June 1881, King Steam is saying to King Coal about the baby, Electricity, 'What will he grow to?'

■ *Did the artist think that a shortage of energy was likely? (The 'baby' is holding a jar labelled 'storage of force'. At that time the word 'force' was used where we would use 'energy')*

Source 218 Plenty more oil

The petroleum is abundant and more will be formed in the earth while the supply of pine-wood may be exhausted.
(Shen Kuo. China, AD 1070)

About the year 1800, however, the modern scientific ideas about geology and the formation of fossils began to be worked out. By 1850 these ideas were widely accepted. So some people suggested that coal reserves might eventually be used up just as some forests had been. To most people this was not a very serious danger.

Source 219 Enough for 1200 years?

When one tree is cut down to be burned, another can be planted in its room, but when once a stratum of coal is removed no-one could think that it will grow again. People have attempted to foretell the period when the mines at present known or guessed at in this island will be completely exhausted: when Britons shall be obliged to get a supply from abroad if such a supply is to be found. If not, like their ancestors they must resort to wood or turf, to say nothing of the dried horse and sheep dung made use of by some of the poor in certain districts of our own islands at this day. Fortunately, however, for our comfort, none of these calculations place the period nearer than many hundred years: some extend it as far as twelve hundred years

and even two thousand years. We may, therefore, for our part, be pretty much at ease on the subject, and leave our posterity to shift for themselves.
(C. Gray: *Early Trades and Industries,* 1808)

Source 220 No limit to the energies of nature

. . . Fears as to the possible exhaustion of our coal mines are entirely groundless. If the present consumption of coal be estimated at 16 million of tons annually, it is demonstrated that the coalfields of the country would not be exhausted for many centuries.

We may safely assume that long before such a period of time shall have rolled away other more powerful mechanical agents will supersede the use of coal. Philosophy has already directed her finger at sources of inexhaustible power in electricity and magnetism.

We are on the eve of mechanical discoveries still greater than any which have yet appeared. The steam engine itself will dwindle into insignificance in comparison with the energies of nature which are still to be released.
(Dr. Lardner: *On the Steam Engine,* 1840)

■ *Why was Dr. Lardner, writing in 1840, so sure that new sorts of energy would be found?*

One or two people took a more pessimistic view. One such person was Professor W. Jevons, writing 25 years after Dr. Lardner.

Source 221 Britain will run out of coal by the 20th century

Coal is like a spring wound up during geological ages for us to let down.

(What other fuels could Britain use when the coal is exhausted?) . . .

I have calculated that forests of an extent two and a half times exceeding the whole area of the United Kingdom would be required to furnish the . . . equivalent to our coal production.

Petroleum has of late become the matter of a most extensive trade, and has even been proposed by American inventors for use in steam engine boilers. It is undoubtedly superior to coal for some purposes and is capable of replacing it . . . But then its natural supply is far more limited and uncertain than that of coal.

It is just possible that some day sunbeams may be collected or that some source of energy now unknown may be detected. But such a discovery would simply destroy our industrial supremacy. (Professor W. Jevons: *The Coal Question,* 1865)

- *Who was proved right? Dr. Lardner or Professor Jevons?*

Most people paid little attention to such arguments. During this period new reserves of coal and oil were discovered in many parts of the world. Railways, pipelines and oil tankers made it possible to carry fuel cheaply over great distances. The coming of electricity and the internal combustion engine meant that energy could be taken nearly anywhere at little cost. So why should people worry about shortages?

Even at this time of plenty, there were fuel shortages for some people.

Source 222 Cooking in Lambeth, 1910

Another difficulty which dogs the path of a Lambeth housewife is either that there is no oven or only a gas oven which requires a good deal of gas. Homes where there is no oven send out to the bakehouse on Sunday. The rest of the week is managed on cold food, or the hard-worked saucepan and frying pan are brought into play. An economical stove or fireplace is out of reach of the poor. They are often obliged to use old-fashioned and broken ranges and grates which devour coal with as little benefit to the user as possible. They are driven to cook by gas, which ought to be an excellent way of cooking, but under the penny-in-the-slot system it is a way which tends to underdone food.

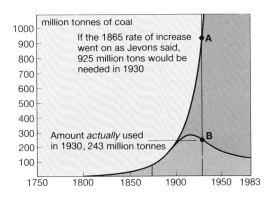

A graph of coal used in Britain, based on one drawn by Professor Jevons in 1865

million tonnes of coal

If the 1865 rate of increase went on as Jevons said, 925 million tons would be needed in 1930 — A

Amount *actually* used in 1930, 243 million tonnes — B

Source 223 Advertisement, 1892. Heaters like this were widely used in California and Arizona about 1900

Mr. P., printer's labourer. Six children. Average wage 24s. (£1.20) Allowed his wife £1 in the week. 1–7 Dec. 1910.

Mrs. P.'s budget:

Rent	8s.0d. (40p)
Insurance	1s.8d. (8.5p)
Coal	1s.6d. (7.5p)
Wood	3d. (1.25p)
Gas	1s.0d. (5p)
Boot club	1s.0d. (5p)
Soap etc.	6d. (2.5p)
Blacking	1d. (0.4p)
Cotton and tapes	3d. (1.25p)
Food	5s.9d. (28.75p)

(M. Pember Reeves: *Round About a Pound a Week,* 1913)

- *During this period there seemed to be plenty of energy. Why did some people still try to conserve it by using it efficiently?*

- *Why didn't the poor people of Lambeth do this?*

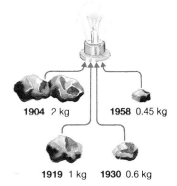

1904 2 kg   1958 0.45 kg

1919 1 kg   1930 0.6 kg

This diagram shows the coal needed to make *one* unit of electricity in the most economical power station at various dates

World coal
production 1983
4 thousand
million tonnes

WORLD COAL RESERVES 1983
1000 thousand million tonnes

World coal production and known reserves, 1983

Since 1945: A world shortage?

The world used up as much fossil fuel in the years 1945–70 as in the whole of history before that. Most of this was oil or natural gas.

The geologists do not know how much of these fuels is left in the ground, but they all agree that they are being used up much faster than they are being discovered.

Source 224 A new North Sea oilfield needed every year

Prospects of finding more 'super giant' fields are receding. In the previous three decades they accounted for the greater part of the increase in oil production. To maintain the present level of production requires the discovery, every year, of two Alaskas, or as much oil as has been found in the North Sea in the last ten years.
(BP *Oil Crisis . . . again?* 1978)

Nobody thinks that the world supplies of oil and gas will suddenly stop. But everybody agrees that they will become scarcer. When goods are scarce the price goes up, and in the 1970s the price of oil went up from $3 a barrel to $30. It seems possible that soon after the year 2000, oil and gas might become too scarce and expensive to use as fuel.

In sixteenth-century Britain, when wood supplies began to run short, people had used coal instead. Perhaps coal could come back into use as the main fuel of the high energy civilisation?

- *How long would the 1983 reserves of coal last at the 1983 rate of production?*

- *Could coal be used for all the purposes for which oil is used?*

As fuel prices rise it becomes more worth while to explore for new coal or oil reserves. So some new reserves of fossil fuels are certain to be discovered.

- *Can this be done fast enough to go on meeting the world energy need?*

Part of this graph is a guess about the future.

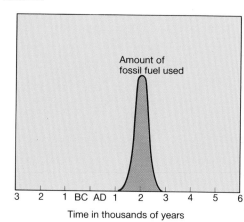

Amount of
fossil fuel used

Time in thousands of years

Source 225 From M. Gabel *Energy, Earth and Everyone*, 1980

- *Does it fit in with the evidence given at the top of the page and on page 82?*

What about nuclear energy?

At the same time as the world was beginning to face the possibility of a shortage of fossil fuels, a new source of energy, uranium, was coming into use. One tonne of uranium can produce as much electricity as 20000 tonnes of coal in today's power stations. Would nuclear energy solve the problem?

The nuclear reactors in use at present (1984) can only use 0.7 per cent of the natural uranium. The rest is wasted. Many countries are working hard to develop another type of reactor, the 'fast reactor'. Scientists have shown that in a reactor of this type, the other 99.3 per cent of the uranium could be turned into plutonium and then be used as reactor fuel. One tonne of uranium would then produce the electrical energy of 1500000 tonnes of coal. It is not yet certain how much it will cost to build and run a power station using this process. The first ones are likely to come into use in the 1980s. If the process is a commercial success it will make the world's uranium last about 60 times as long.

- *Is nuclear power likely to solve the world energy problem?*

The atom to the rescue

The Soviet Union is the first country in the world to start using the atom to provide everyday domestic heat. Two cities, Voronezh and Gorky, are already building atomic heat-and-power stations which meet all safety requirements. By 1990 many other populous parts of the country will have them. This will save up to a third of the country's present oil output, estimated at 593 million tons this year. Moreover, heat from the atom will cost only half as much as heat produced by burning solid fuel.

Sooner or later nuclear energy must form the basis of the world economy. Only the atom is capable of meeting its peoples' growing needs. In the next 10–12 years the total capacity of Soviet atomic power stations is to be raised to 100 million kilowatts. They will save each year more than 170 million tons of solid fuel or over 120 million tons of oil.

Source 226 From *Soviet Weekly*, 22 September 1979

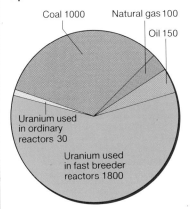

Amount of energy available in thousand million tonnes of oil equivalent

Coal 1000 Natural gas 100 Oil 150 Uranium used in ordinary reactors 30 Uranium used in fast breeder reactors 1800

World reserves of various forms of energy, 1981

Uranium mine bid

The Central Electricity Board has made an estimated £150 millions bid for a half share in an uranium mining project in Australia.

Source 227 From the *Guardian*, 3 October 1979

Energy policy: What has been done?

In the 1960s most countries set up a special government department to deal with the energy problem. The oil companies and other business firms have also started to think about it. So have many ordinary people. The rise in prices forced many of them to try to use less energy.

As in earlier times of shortage people are looking for new sources of energy and trying to conserve existing ones.

Many houses and flats were built when energy was cheaper. People found that they could not afford the high prices in the 1970s and 1980s.

Developing new supplies of energy

1 Conventional sources

Source 228 The largest power station in the world, Brazil. The Itaipu hydro-electric station on the Rio Parana between Brazil and Paraguay. It produces 12 600 MW of electric power

2 Unconventional sources

Source 229 A wind-powered generator

British research into wave energy

Hot water test drill a success

Britain's first attempt to tap a reservoir of hot water deep down in the earth's crust to use as an energy source has proved a success, the Junior Energy Minister, Mr John Moore, announced yesterday.

The £1.8 million well, at Marchwood, near Southampton, found water at 5,500 ft. Allowing for heat loss in transit, the water will come to the surface at a temperature of 65–67 degrees centigrade. There is sufficient to heat about 1,000 homes for several decades.

Source 230 From the *Guardian*, 25 April 1980

Source 231 Xiao Han, a Chinese Government Official, in *Economic Reporter*, Hong Kong, February 1981

China puts coal and hydro-electricity first

In order to accelerate the development of China's energy industry, the Party Central Committee decided to give priority to coal and hydro-power. In addition actions will be taken for the exploration for new oil wells. In regions lacking energy resources, preparations will be made to build nuclear-power stations and to develop marsh gas in the countryside. Old coal mines with rich reserves will be expanded.

Source 232 From the *Guardian*, 9 May 1980

More research on 'natural' energy

By David Fairhall, Energy Editor

For every pound the Department of Energy has spent on supporting research into 'renewable' sources of energy – such as solar, wind and wave power – the Government has put £60 into the nuclear power programmes. But the research budget for renewable sources has trebled since last year.

Fuel from crops and organic waste, the so-called biofuels, are rated by the department as 'a significant energy resource', which could produce the energy equivalent to 60 million tons of coal a year. Wave energy is described in the review as 'a substantial energy resource'. Solar water heating could contribute the annual equivalent in energy of between one and four million tons of coal by the end of the century, the department estimates.

This sun-powered furnace in the French Pyrenees reaches a temperature of 3300 °C

Source 235 Tidal power station across the estuary of the River Rance in Brittany. The tide operates the turbines as it flows and ebbs

Conservation of existing supplies

Go-ahead for first power station to recycle waste heat for industry

Britain's first purpose-built power station designed to sell the waste heat from electricity generation to power nearby industries has been approved by the Department of Energy. It will be sited in Hereford and built by the Midlands Electricity Board at a cost of £3.5m.

Source 233 From *The Times*, 22 February 1978

Source 234 From *The Times*, 17 January 1984

Chinese plan for conservation

The State Council has decided to stress both exploration and conservation of energy resources. In the short term, priority will be given to conservation. They plan that the amount of energy to be conserved annually in the five years of the Sixth Five Year Plan period will be the equivalent of 24 million tonnes of standard coal.

Source 236 Xiao Han, a Chinese government official, in *Economic Reporter*, Hong Kong, February 1981

Factory saves £25,000 on energy

An energy economy drive at the York factory of Joseph Terry and Sons Ltd is yielding savings estimated at £25,000 this year.

Savings range from improvements in the efficiency of production machines to reductions in the power of lamps used for floodlighting.

The firm's main energy source is gas, costing £300,000 a year, and a target has been set to cut this by 10 percent.

Source 237 From the *Yorkshire Evening Press*, 28 June 1979

Hard-headed return to the age of sailing

By Michael Baily, Transport Editor

Britain re-enters the age of sail this week with the launch of the first ocean-going wind-powered cargo ship for half a century.

A 400-tonner, she will from March ply the old trade route from Britain down the west coast of Africa and across to the Caribbean, then back on a more northerly route to catch the trade winds.

With a 100-ft steel hull and twin 100-ft masts, the ship is expected to maintain a steady speed of 8½ knots saving around £11,000 on fuel bills.

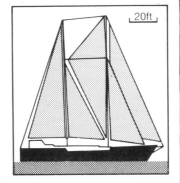

How the clipper will look

- *In what ways is the problem of shortage and the need for conservation quite different in the 1980s from earlier periods?*

- *In what ways are the problems the same?*

- *Which methods used to deal with the problems are the same as in earlier periods?*

- *What new methods are being used?*

9 Government and energy

Who made the decisions about energy? Who decided whether new methods like water mills or nuclear power stations should be used or not?

Sometimes it has been the government of a country. Sometimes business men or other groups of people have been more important. Sometimes we have no evidence about who made the decisions. The decision to use fire, or to harness animals, for instance, must have been taken by many separate people at different times and places when they first saw how useful these things were.

To work out what influence governments have had on the history of energy, you should ask:

- *When have governments taken an active part in decisions about energy?*

- *Have they tried to: **a)** control existing supplies? **b)** find new supplies? **c)** prevent pollution? **d)** make sure energy is used safely?*

- *Why have they tried to do these things?*

- *When have important decisions been taken by other people, like business men, and not by governments?*

- *How important a factor has government policy been?*

Low energy civilisations

Source 238 Gangs of labourers moving a statue. From a tomb carving, Egypt, about 2000 BC

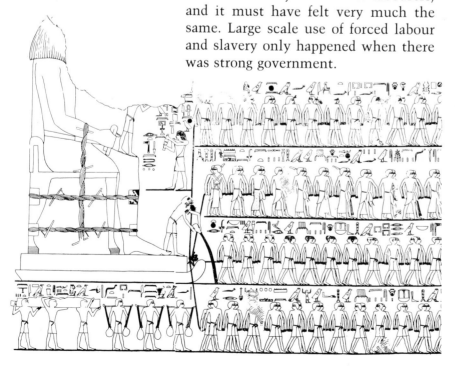

Governments use of slavery and forced labour

Most people in the early cities were not slaves. But many were forced labourers, and it must have felt very much the same. Large scale use of forced labour and slavery only happened when there was strong government.

Source 239 Jews forced to labour in Egypt

The Egyptians made the children of Israel serve with rigour. And they made their lives bitter with hard bondage in mortar and in brick and in all manner of service in the field. All their service wherein they made them serve was with rigour.

And Pharoah commanded the taskmasters of the people, saying 'Ye shall no more give to the people straw to make bricks. Let them go and gather the straw for themselves. And the number of bricks which they did make ye shall not diminish. For they be idle. This is why they cry out saying "Let us go and sacrifice to our God." Let there be more work laid upon the men'. (*Exodus.*)

This account was first compiled about 800 BC. The events took place about 1300 BC.

■ *What do you think the soldiers in the picture on the right are for?*

Government controls of energy use

Energy has sometimes caused problems for governments. These were not as serious during times of low energy use as they have become in the last hundred years, but the problems were often similar.

Source 240 No furnaces allowed near the Palace

From the Emperors Honorius and Theodosius to Aetius, Prefect of the City (Constantinople, capital of the eastern half of the Roman Empire). We order the removal of all furnaces throughout the entire space that extends along the shore of the sea between the amphitheatre and the port of Saint Julia. We do this for the sake of the healthfulness of our most noble city and on account of the nearness of our palace. No licence shall be granted to any person to burn lime in those places.
(Order made 4 October AD 419. From the Laws of Roman Emperor Theodosius)

Source 241 Compulsory supply of fuel

When charcoal is required for the minting of money or for necessary manufacture of arms, no-one shall be excused from supplying it.
(Order of the Roman Emperors Valentinian and Theodosius, 5 July AD 390).

Source 242 No coal to be used

The King learns from the complaints of the prelates and magnates of his realm who often come to London . . . and of his citizens and all his people dwelling there . . . that the workmen now burn (lime-kilns) and construct them of sea-coal instead of brushwood or charcoal. From the use of this sea-coal an unbearable smell diffuses itself throughout the neighbouring places and the air is greatly affected, to the annoyance of citizens and others and the injury of their bodily health . . . so the use of coal is forbidden.
(Proclamation by King Edward II of England, 1307)

Source 243 Fined for cutting wood

Fines of Longdendale. (The Jury) swear on their oath that John Robinson, Thomas Robinson, Robert Booth, William Bebye (and 11 others) did cut the green wood of Our Lady the Queen in the Combes.
(Court Roll of the High Peak, Derbyshire, 1583). Fines ranging from 2d. to 8d. (1p. to 3.5p) were imposed.

■ *What kinds of energy problems did governments in the low energy civilisations face?*

■ *What steps did they take to deal with these problems?*

Non-government control of energy use

When there was a shortage or pollution, governments often tried to control fuel or the ways people used it. But many of the most important decisions were made by people or groups of people who had nothing to do with the government.

■ *Who took the decisions to build watermills and windmills in the Middle Ages: a) the King, b) the barons, c) the abbots, d) the millers, or e) the peasants?*

Source 244 This drawing was made in AD 1833. It is from the autobiography of a Chinese canal engineer. Most of the canal system of China was completed by the Chinese government about 1000 years before the date of this drawing. The methods shown here were all in use then. The people working here are not slaves, but peasants forced to work by government officials

123

High energy civilisations

Businessmen become more important

Who made the important decisions that led to the Industrial Revolution? Steam engines, coal mines and railways were very expensive. People had to be prepared to risk large sums of money before these things could be built. Watt's steam engine is a good example. The first person to invest money in it, Dr John Roebuck, went bankrupt in 1773. He estimated that it would cost another £10000 to complete the engine. In fact it cost Matthew Boulton, Watt's next partner, £47000. Boulton was a very rich and successful man, and was able to borrow money from London banks, but it took him ten years to pay it off.

It was the same with large cotton mills, coal mines, railways and steamships. Before these things could be built large amounts of capital were needed. For example from 1826 to 1846 a total of £153,000,000 was invested by shareholders in the new British railway companies. A special Act of Parliament was needed to build a railway which ran across public roads and across other peoples' land. But apart from this the government took little part in the decisions to build steam engines, coal mines, factories, railways and steamships which made Britain the first high energy country in the world.

■ *Who took the main decisions at this time:* **a)** *inventors* **b)** *businessmen or* **c)** *people who lent money or bought shares?*

The United States Government attacks the Standard Oil Company in 1911

J.D. Rockefeller built up his huge oil company by buying out his rivals or driving them out of business by selling oil cheaper than they could. Several rival companies agreed to join with Rockefeller in a 'Trust', a monster firm which could fix prices. After a few years this Trust controlled nearly all American oil – it was a monopoly. In 1899 it made a profit of $45 million.

American business men had done the same thing in other industries like steel or railways. During the years 1880–1900 a tiny group of such men came to control the most important American industries.

Many Americans were horrified to see so much power in the hands of a few rich men. Some argued that monopolies prevented free competition between business men. Some argued that by raising prices they were robbing ordinary folk to make a few people very rich indeed. Public opinion was strong enough to force through a series of laws against the trusts between 1896 and 1914. In a famous case in 1911 the US Supreme Court ordered the Standard

Table 4 **The world's richest companies, 1981**

		Turnover in millions US dollars	Country
1	Exxon (formerly Eastern Standard Oil)	108108	United States
2	Royal Dutch Shell	77834	Anglo-Dutch
3	Mobil	64448	United States
4	General Motors	62699	United States
5	Texaco	57628	United States
6	British Petroleum	49192	United Kingdom
7	Standard Oil California	44224	United States
8	Ford Motor	38247	United States
9	Standard Oil Indiana	29947	United States
10	IBM	29070	United States
11	Kuwait Petroleum	28720	Kuwait
12	Gulf Oil	28252	United States
13	Atlantic Richfield	27797	United States
14	ENI	27724	Italy
15	General Electric	27240	United States
16	Du Pont de Nemours	22810	United States
17	Unilever	22707	Anglo-Dutch
18	Shell Oil	21629	United States
19	VEBA	22045	West Germany
20	Total Oil	21632	France

Oil Company to be broken up into 38 separate parts, which were not to be allowed to agree secretly together.

This did not lead to a fall in the price of oil, and it did not stop the owners of oil companies getting very rich.

It did, however, make it easier for new oil companies to be formed. Perhaps this helped to encourage competition. The 'Anti-Trust' laws are still in force in the USA.

- *How many of the companies shown in the table on page 124 are oil companies? How many are American?*

- *How many were originally part of Rockefeller's company?*

- *What conclusions can be drawn from this list about the success of the anti-trust laws?*

- *What conclusions can be drawn about the power and importance of oil companies?*

The British Government buys part of an oil company, 1914

In 1911 Winston Churchill became First Lord of the Admiralty, in charge of the Navy. It was a time when a naval war with Germany seemed possible, and both countries were building battle-ships as fast as they could. Churchill's experts told him that it would be much better to use oil as the fuel in bat-tleships, instead of coal.

Source 245 A difficult decision
On my arrival at the Admiralty we were not dependent upon oil . . .

The advantage conferred by the liquid fuel was inestimable. In equal ships it gave a large excess of speed over coal. It gave 40 per cent greater radius of action for the same weight of fuel. The use of oil made it possible in every type of vessel to have more gun-power and more speed for less size and cost.

But oil is not to be found in appreciable quantities in our islands. If we require it we must carry it by sea in peace or war from distant countries. We had, on the other hand, the finest supply of the best steam

coal in the world safe in our mines under our own hand.

To change the foundation of the Navy from British coal to foreign oil . . . there must be accumulated in Great Britain an enormous oil reserve . . . Fleets of tankers had to be built to carry the oil from the distant oil fields.

The oil supplies of the world were at this time in the hands of vast oil trusts under foreign control.
(W.S. Churchill: *The World Crisis*, 1923)

- *Who was Churchill thinking of in his last sentence?*

In 1914, after talking for a long time with the oil companies Churchill arranged for the British Government to buy 51 per cent of the shares in a new British company 'Anglo-Persian Oil'. Later it changed its name to BP. This gave the Government power to control the company, so it could be sure of getting the oil it needed at a reasonable price.

- *In the nineteenth century governments let business men make decisions about energy. Why did governments interfere more in these decisions in the twentieth century?*

Source 246 German battleship loading coal, 1916.

- *What advantage would oil have, from the sailor's point of view?*

Governments take greater control

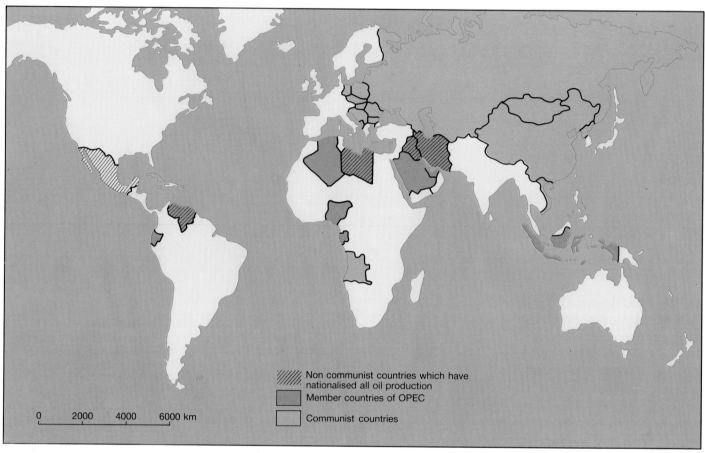

Non communist countries which have nationalised all oil production
Member countries of OPEC
Communist countries

0   2000   4000   6000 km

Government control of energy

Some governments have complete control

The communist countries have a 'state controlled' system. All important industry has been 'nationalised', or brought into public ownership so it can be controlled completely by the government. This applies to the energy industries: mines, oil wells, power stations and pipe lines. Fuel prices are fixed by the government. Russia was the first country to adopt communism, in 1917. The communists argue that their system is the only way of making sure that things are run in the interests of *all* the people and not for the benefit of a small class of rich property owners, the 'capitalists'.

Some governments have little control

The USA and many other countries have a 'private enterprise' system. Industry is owned by the shareholders of large companies or corporations. Many Americans believe that the best way of making sure that there is plenty for everyone is to allow businessmen as much freedom as possible, and for the government to interfere with their decisions as little as possible. Most mines, power stations and oil wells are privately owned.

But even in the USA, the government of President Roosevelt decided in 1933 to build and run power stations and sell electricity in a large area of the USA. This was done to try to cure the massive unemployment. The government body set up to do this, the Tennessee Valley Authority, was very successful and still exists.

The US Government also makes regulations about safety and pollution which the privately-owned companies have to obey.

Some governments have partial control

Most West European countries, and many in other parts of the world, have 'mixed economies'. Some industries have been nationalised, and some are owned by private companies. In Britain for instance, the Labour Government of 1945–51 nationalised the coal mines and the gas and electricity industries.

In most countries with mixed economies, the coal, gas and electricity industries have been nationalised. This was partly because of the ideas of the socialists in these countries. They thought that the system of private ownership of industry gave too much power to the rich, and at times caused large scale unemployment and distress for the poor.

They argued that this could be put right if the government took over full control of a few important parts of industry. They could leave the rest in private ownership, but control it enough to prevent unemployment or unfairness.

There was another reason for the nationalisation of electricity in these and other countries. Except in the very largest countries like the USA there could only be one electricity system. It would be very wasteful to built two sets of power stations and supply systems to compete with one another. Also power stations, particularly hydro-electric stations with their huge dams, cost so much to build that only the government could provide the money. So if there could only be one system, and the government had to pay for it, it seemed best that the government should own it.

Governments take control of oil

Many of the new oil fields found in the twentieth century were in poor countries. The people of these countries often resented the power of the big American and British oil companies. As the governments of these oil producing countries learned more about the oil business, they began to demand a bigger share for themselves. They wanted to be able to fix prices and decide on the amount of oil to produce. One way to do this was to nationalise the oil industry completely. The first country to do this was Mexico in 1938. Many others have done so since then.

Source 247 Hands off our oil

We as the owners of this oil and the masters of this land, must have a say in the production of this wealth because the needs of this country are clear. No firm, no company, no organisation can tell us. 'We will produce and export so much of your national wealth, but you cannot touch the rest because we do not wish to use it.' They want to deprive Iran of this wealth which rightfully belongs to us.
(The Shah of Iran, 14 March 1968.)

OPEC (The Organisation of Petroleum Exporting Countries)

In 1960 a group of oil producing governments began to combine to make a better bargain with the big oil companies. In the 1970s the 13 countries of OPEC forced the oil companies to agree to large increases in crude oil prices.

Fort Loudon Dam, Tennessee, being built for the Tennessee Valley Authority, 1938

Government controls on how energy is used

1 Pollution controls

Governments have tried to deal with pollution since Roman times. The problems became much more serious in the high energy civilisation of the last 100 years, and more government action was taken. Sometimes this was succesful. (See the pictures below.) Sometimes governments are less successful.

Source 248 Sulphuric acid in the rain

Britain is to be pressed by Norway to join an international conference next year on pollution which Norway claims is coming from the industrial centres of Europe and affecting her water supplies.

Sulphur dioxide from power stations in the UK, West and East Germany and Poland, is alleged to be carried to Scandinavia before being dumped on the ground as rainfall. Norway has called for E.E.C. action for several years, but without success.

(*The Guardian*, 27 April 1978)

■ *Why is it difficult to control pollution of this kind?*

Longton, Staffordshire, in 1910 and 1970. This change was due partly to the Clean Air Act of 1956. This compelled factories and householders in British towns to use smokeless fuel, and helped them to pay for more efficient grates and boilers

2 Control by taxes

One way of limiting the amount of energy people use is to make it cost more. In Britain and many other countries the taxes on some sources of energy are very high. These taxes are a way of getting money for governments, but they also have important effects on which fuels people decide to use.

- *If these taxes did not exist, what effect would there be on the cost of petrol?*

There are no similar taxes on coal, gas or nuclear energy. In fact many governments pay out subsidies to make coal cheaper and to help to build nuclear power stations.

- *Why might governments tax some sources of energy like oil and subsidise some others like coal?*

3 Control for conservation

In the 1970s it became clear that there was likely to be a world shortage of energy, especially oil. Most governments in the high energy countries began to make plans to deal with it.

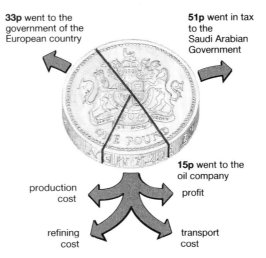

33p went to the government of the European country

51p went in tax to the Saudi Arabian Government

15p went to the oil company profit

production cost

profit

refining cost

transport cost

Where does the money go? What happened to every pound spent by a motorist in Europe on petrol from Saudi Arabian oil in 1980

4 Governments pay for research

One way of dealing with the oil problem was to encourage the development of nuclear power. All earlier new forms of power had first been developed by inventors and business men, like Watt and Boulton. But the early research and development of nuclear power was organised and paid for by governments.

- *Why might today's governments be more willing to spend money on new forms of energy than those of earlier times?*

Source 249 *The Observer*, 19 February 1978

Study shows that fuel bills can be cut

The first Government-controlled experiments on domestic energy are expected to demonstrate that bills can be cut by 20 per cent.

This is much less than the ideal of the Watts Committee, part of the Government's Advisory Council on Energy Conservation, which has calculated that energy savings of up to 88 per cent are possible.

But it is enough to encourage the Government's energy planners in their current programme of spending £100 million to bring two million council homes up to a minimum standard of thermal insulation over 10 years.

The forthcoming results, which are being processed by a computer at Bristol University and are expected to be published soon, are based on a study throughout three winters of 40 council houses in Plymouth.

Twenty of the houses were insulated with four inches of insulating wool in the roof and foam in the wall cavities. Twenty identical houses on the same estate, built to Government regulations but having no extra insulation are being used as 'control' houses.

A government leaflet offering grants to householders to insulate their homes

There are government and other schemes which could help you with your fuel bills and heating costs. This leaflet is a quick guide to what help is available and where you can get more information.

HELP WITH INSULATING YOUR HOME

Insulating your loft and draught-stripping doors and windows are the best ways to hold down the cost of keeping your home warm. You may be eligible for help towards the cost of some forms of home insulation.

INSULATION

10

Ideas and the history of energy

This section deals with some of the ideas that have been important in the history of energy. The most obvious one is science. Modern nuclear energy, for instance, could not have been developed without a knowledge of atomic physics.

What ideas about energy were held before the coming of modern science? What effects did they have on the history of energy? To be successful, hunter-gatherers needed a detailed knowledge of animals, and the right mixture of respect for them and fear for their power. It was the same with fire.

Where did it come from? How could it be controlled? The earliest answers to these questions were probably a mixture of common sense and religious beliefs.

In using this section, ask:

- *What ideas have been important in the history of energy?*

- *How did ideas slow down change and how did they speed it up?*

- *What changes in the use of energy could not take place unless changes in people's ideas took place first?*

Magical and religious ideas in early times

Source 250 A Yanomami tribesman from the Amazon lighting a fire with a fire drill. Modern photographs

Who first made fire?

Fire is strange and powerful stuff. It can hurt or destroy people, but its warmth can also save their lives. It seems to come from nowhere and disappear into nothing. Many people's have made up stories about how it began, though we have none from prehistoric times.

Small pieces of smouldering charcoal could be insulated and kept alight inside a hollow plant stem such as a fennel stalk

Source 253 In revenge Zeus chained Prometheus to a rock. Every day vultures came to tear out his liver. Prometheus is shown on the right on this Laconian cup from Sparta, about 6th century BC

Source 251 A cat-man made fire

The maker of fire was Yigaurara, a cat-man. Being laughed at by the people, he made fire and burned them all up. The myth is associated with a mass of black stones which are said to be the remains of the people who were burned. The fire is said to travel inside the ground, and to come out a long way off, and so, whenever fire breaks out suddenly and unaccountably, it can be referred to as the fire started by Yigaurara.

Songs commemorate Yigaurara's doings at fire-making and fire-spreading. The song for making fire by twirling is: 'Neka takaaba balu rari inya'.'Neka' is fire, and 'takaaba' refers to the twirling of the sticks; the other words are 'the song'.

For the Aborigines life without the firestick is unthinkable: to sit down or to sleep by day or night without it is almost impossible. It is often used as the symbol of marriage; the burning points of two firesticks are made to touch and are kept touching until the sticks are both burned away; this symbolises the common fire of man and wife and also their common life. The newly circumcized youth is left with his fire, with the implication that from now on he may make and be responsible for fire. (A.P. Elkin: *The Australian Aborigines*, 1938)

One very common myth is that fire was brought from heaven. Prometheus was a man but also son of the god Iapetos. Before the fire story begins he has played a trick on Zeus, the ruler of the gods.

Source 252 Fire stolen from the gods

Zeus, the gatherer of the clouds, was furious. 'Son of Iapetos, cleverest god of all! So, friend, you do not yet forget your crafty tricks!' Thus spoke the angry Zeus. From that time Zeus remembered the trick and would not give to wretched men who live on earth, the power of fire which never wearies.

The brave son of Iapetos deceived him, and stole the ray of unwearied fire and hid it in a hollow fennel stalk. Zeus, who thunders in the heavens, ate his heart and raged within to see the ray of fire among men. (Hesiod: *Theogony*, Greece, eighth century BC)

- *Beliefs similar to these were quite common all over the world in ancient times and amongst uncivilised peoples more recently. Why might people make up such stories?*

- *Would the hunter-gatherers of the Old Stone Age have held similar beliefs?*

Temple of Vesta

Altar with holy flame

Source 254 A Roman coin, third century AD. Vesta was the Roman goddess of the hearth. The sacred fire was said to have been brought from Troy when Rome was founded. It was kept burning by six Vestal Virgins. They took a vow of chastity and if they broke it or let the fire go out, they were punished

Fire rituals: using fire with respect

The idea that fire was part of the world of the gods was very common. It would only serve man if he treated it with proper respect. Otherwise things might go wrong. People might be burned or the things they were making or doing might be spoiled. So they often followed out a careful set of rules as exactly as they could.

Source 255 Religion at the glassworks

(To make glass) Thou shalt seek out a favourable day in a favourable month. In the house of the furnace thou shalt set figures of the gods. A stranger shall not enter, nor shall one that is unclean tread before them. The day when thou puttest the minerals into the furnace thou shalt make a sacrifice before the gods.

Thou shalt kindle a fire underneath the furnace and shalt put down the minerals. The wood thou shalt burn underneath the furnace shall be styrax wood, thick billets with the bark removed which have been kept in leather coverings, cut in the month of Ab.

Thou shalt crush 10 mana of sand; 15 mana of alkali ash; 1⅔ mana of styrax gum. Thou shalt mix them together and put them in the furnace.
(Tablet of King Assurbanipal, Assyria, 668–26 BC)

Source 256 Sacrificing an animal

The method of sacrifice is everywhere the same . . . As soon as the animal is strangled, he is skinned, and then comes the boiling of the flesh. This has called for a little inventiveness, because there is no wood in Scythia (southern Russia) to make a fire with. The method the natives adopt is to strip the flesh from the bones and put it in a cauldron – if, that is, they happen to possess one, and then make a fire of the bones underneath it. In the absence of a cauldron they put all the flesh into the animal's paunch, mix water with it and boil it like that over the bone-fire. The bones burn very well, and the paunch easily contains all the meat once it has been stripped off. In this way the ox or any other sacrifical beast is made to boil itself. When the meat is cooked, the sacrificer offers a portion of the flesh and entrails by throwing it upon the ground in front of him. All sorts of cattle are offered in sacrifice, but most commonly horses.
(Herodotus: *Histories*, c.450 BC)

- *Ideas, rituals and sacrifices like these were very common throughout the ancient world. What practical value might they have for the people who used them?*

- *What other reasons could there be for their use over a very long period?*

Greek and Roman ideas

Between about 600 BC–AD 100, Greek thinkers began to look at nature in a new way. The main idea was that people could make sense of the natural world by thinking hard and working things out. This was because, like people, the natural world obeyed laws which people could understand, if they followed the rules for correct thinking. For instance, the Greeks asked the simple question, 'What are the basic elements out of which things are made?' The answer they gave was that everything was made out of four elements; earth, water, fire and air. Fire is the lightest and moves naturally upwards, perhaps towards the sun. Earth is the heaviest, and moves naturally downwards.

The Greeks worked out ideas which fitted so well together that they were accepted as correct for nearly 2000 years. Then in the seventeenth century, the founders of modern science proved many of the Greek ideas to be wrong. But the Greek idea of a clear and logical enquiry to find the truth, continues to be the basis of modern science.

One important reason for the success of the Greeks was their use of mathematics, particularly geometry.

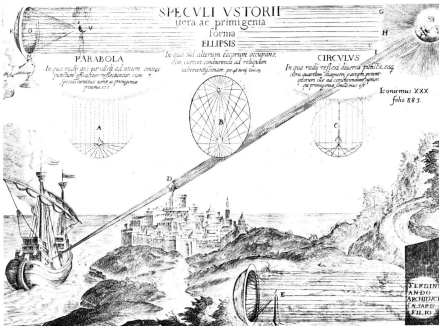

Source 258 Engraving from *The Great Art of Light and Darkness* by A. Kircher, Germany, 1646. The story of using the sun's rays to burn ships had also been told in Roman times. It is impossible to start a fire at any distance using this method

For instance, in the third century BC Eratosthenes used mathematical arguments and some quite simple observation, to work out the diameter of the earth. His figure was 12 560 kilometres. The correct value is 12 682 kilometres!

During the second century BC the Greek mathematician Diocles had shown how a parabolic mirror focussed the rays of the sun to light a fire. This made it far easier to design a burning mirror that really worked. The Romans used one to light the sacred lamp.

The Greek theory of the four elements fitted in with common-sense observation

Source 257 How to light the holy flame

The sacred lamp is said to have been put out . . . at Rome in the War of Mithridates (first century BC.) and also in the Civil War (44 BC), when not only was the fire extinguished but the altar overturned. It is not to be lighted again from another fire, but new fire is to be gained by drawing down a pure and unpolluted flame from the sunbeams. They generally kindle it with a concave vessel of brass . . . This being placed against the sun causes its rays to converge in the centre, which, by reflection acquiring the force and activity of fire, rarify the air and immediately kindle such light matter as they think fit to apply.
(Plutarch: *Lives*, Rome, 1st century AD)

133

Alexandria

Most Greek thinkers were not interested in practical matters like better burning mirrors. In most parts of the Greek world there were no machines more complicated than an ox cart or a potter's wheel. These were used by slaves and craftsmen, not by scholars.

One place where some learned Greeks did take an interest in machines was Alexandria. The Greeks under Alexander the Great had conquered Egypt and set up a university at Alexandria in about 300BC. In its library it could collect together the knowledge of the whole civilised world, even perhaps some from China. Eratosthenes worked here, and so did Archimedes (287–212 BC). Archimedes worked out the mathematics of levers, pulleys and screws. He is said to have invented the compound pulley and other lifting devices. These machines enabled people to apply the energy of human muscles or perhaps of animals more effectively.

Evidence of what was to be a much more important development – the first use of water power, dates from about 100 years after the death of Archimedes.

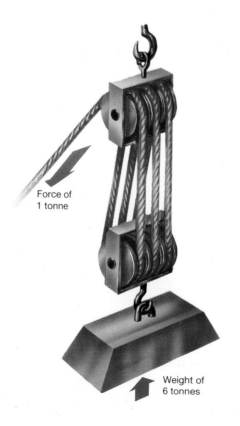

With a compound pulley like this, a pull of one tonne could, in theory, lift six tonnes. Archimedes made calculations like this and may have invented the compound pulley

Force of 1 tonne

Weight of 6 tonnes

- *Could the work of Archimedes and other Greek thinkers have speeded up invention of the water wheel?*

- *What influence did the new Greek way of thinking about nature have on the history of energy in Greek and Roman times?*

Ideas about machines in Medieval Europe

In the Middle Ages the people of Europe got used to machines in a way that no earlier people had ever done.

Source 259 Water power in the monastery

The river enters (Clairvaux) Abbey . . . It gushes first into the corn mill where it is very actively employed in grinding grain under the weight of the wheels and in shaking the fine sieve which separates the flour from the bran. Then it flows into the next building and fills the boiler to prepare beer . . . But the river's work is not yet finished for it is drawn into the fulling machines. There it raises and lowers alternately the heavy hammers or mallets of the fulling machines. Now it enters the tannery where it devotes much care and energy to preparing the necessary materials for the monks' footwear. Then it divides into many small branches and passes through the various departments seeking everywhere for those who require its services for cooking, rotating, crushing, watering, washing or grinding, always offering its help and never refusing. At last, to earn full thanks and to leave nothing undone it carries away the refuse and eaves all clean.

(Ernald, Abbot of Bonnevalle: *Life of St. Bernard*, twelfth century, France).

St. Bernard lived 1090–1153. His Abbey of Clairvaux became the centre of the Cistercian order which included 742 abbeys throughout Europe. They were all built to a similar plan and used water power wherever they could.

- *How many water-powered machines must there have been at Clairvaux Abbey?*

Water- and windmills were built in every village in Europe during the Middle Ages. They were used in iron works and cloth making as well as for grinding corn, so most people would have seen one working. There were thousands of millwrights; craftsmen who could make and repair watermills. The Europeans were becoming 'mechanically minded'.

Source 260 Flying machines are possible

A chariot can be constructed that will move with incalculable speed without any draught animal. Also flying machines may be constructed so that a man may sit in the midst of the machine turning a certain instrument by means of which wings artificially constructed would beat the air like a bird flying. Also a machine of small size may be made for raising and lowering weights of almost infinite amounts.
(Roger Bacon: *On the Secret Works of Nature*, England, thirteenth century)

Roger Bacon (1214–94) was a friar who taught at Oxford University. There is no evidence that he ever tried to make any of the machines he described.

■ *Why should a writer in the Middle Ages even think that such machines were possible?*

■ *None of the machines Roger suggested were built. Does this mean that he has no importance in history?*

Source 261 Illustration from a French fourteenth-century manuscript. The angels turning the handles are keeping the universe moving. Inside the sphere with the fixed stars is that of the sun. Just above the earth is the sphere of the moon. This plan of the universe had been worked out long before by the Greeks in Alexandria.

■ *What can we tell from this drawing about the use of machines in fourteenth-century France?*

Science and the steam engine

Modern science began in Europe in the sixteenth and seventeenth centuries, led by men like Galileo (1564–1642), and Newton (1642–1727). Like the Greeks, they were looking for natural and logical rules or laws to explain why stones fall down but stars and planets don't. But they were different from the Ancient Greeks in two ways. First, they insisted on exact measurement and careful experiments. Second, they were fascinated by the machines they saw around them, and often puzzled about how they worked. Some people in seventeenth century Europe were beginning to think of the universe as an enormous machine, like a clock wound up by God. Perhaps it worked by the same rules as the little machines men could make.

Galileo, Newton and others were at this time working out our modern picture of the Solar System. One part of this picture is that the atmosphere of the earth is only a few hundred miles thick. In between the planets and stars there is an almost complete vacuum. The Greeks had said that a vacuum was quite impossible.

In 1662 Charles II set up the Royal Society, the first scientific society in Britain. It held regular meetings, and published its Transactions to spread new and useful scientific ideas.

Denis Papin was a Frenchman who worked for the Royal Society in the 1680s. He made experiments with a tube (or cylinder) which had a tightly fitting piston sliding up and down inside it. It was very like Guericke's air pump or the water pumps in the mines. Papin filled his cylinder with steam, and then he poured cold water on the outside, so that the steam condensed into water again.

Papin knew that this would make a vacuum inside, and of course the piston was forced in by the pressure of the atmosphere. 'I concluded,' he said, 'that machines could be constructed wherein water, by the help of no very intense heat, and at little cost, could produce a perfect vacuum.' He made no practical use of his idea, though he did use his knowledge of steam to invent the pressure cooker, which he called the 'digester'. In 1688 he went to live in Germany.

A cylinder of the type used by Papin

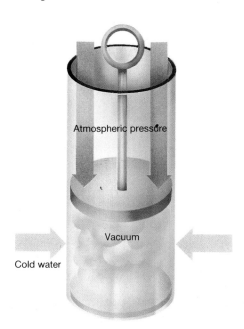

Metal tube or cylinder

Tightly-fitting piston

The cylinder is filled with steam

Atmospheric pressure

Vacuum

Cold water

The Earth from space

In 1702 and in 1712 Savery and Newcomen made the first steam engines. What part did scientific knowledge play in their design?

This question can be answered quite easily in the case of Savery's engine. He was a member of the Royal Society, and was bound to know of the recent work on atmospheric pressure and vacuums. His machine used Papin's idea of filling a container with steam and then condensing it to make a vacuum. But Savery's machine did not work very well. Newcomen's did. Was this because Newcomen knew more science?

To answer this question you should look at the diagram on page 44, which shows how Newcomen's engine worked.

- *Must Newcomen have known about atmospheric pressure and vacuums before he could design such a machine?*

Source 262 **Did Newcomen know any science?**

Now it happened that a man from Dartmouth, named Thomas Newcomen without any knowledge whatever of the speculations of Capt. Savery had at the same time also made up his mind, in conjunction with his assistant, a plumber by the name of Calley, to invent a fire machine for draining water from the mines. He was induced to undertake this by the heavy cost of lifting water by means of horses in the English tin mines. These mines Mr. Newcomen visited in the capacity of dealer in iron tools with which he used to furnish many of the mines. For ten years Mr. Newcomen worked at this fire-machine which would never have worked unless Almighty God had caused an accident to take place. At the last attempt to make the model work the following strange event happened. The cold water, which was allowed to flow into a lead case embracing the cylinder, pierced through an imperfection which had been mended with tin-solder. The heat of the steam caused the tin-solder to melt and thus opened a way for the cold water which rushed into the cylinder and immediately condensed the steam, creating such a vacuum that the air pressed with a tremendous power on the piston. This caused it to crush the bottom of the cylinder as well as the lid of the small boiler. The hot water which flowed everywhere thus convinced the onlookers that they had discovered an incomparably powerful force. Though some might think that this was an accident, I for my part find it impossible to believe this. To this conclusion I – who knew the first inventors – have been brought more than ever when considering that the Almighty then presented mankind with one of the most wonderful inventions which have ever been brought into the light of day, and this by means of ignorant folk who had never acquired a certificate at any University or Academy.

(Martin Triewald, a Swedish engineer: *A Short Description of the Atmospheric Engine*, Stockholm 1734)

Some modern engineers think that the story of the melting solder is unlikely for technical reasons.

- *How reliable is Triewald's evidence?*

- *Was Newcomen's success based upon scientific knowledge?*

Source 263 This picture shows a famous experiment made at Magdeburg, Germany, in 1654. Otto von Guericke was proving the strength of a vacuum. He made an air pump based on the latest design of water pumps for use in the mines. With this he pumped out the air between two metal hemispheres. The pressure of the atmosphere on the outside of the metal was strong enough to hold them together against the pull of sixteen horses. The discovery of the power of atmospheric pressure was to lead within about fifty years to the first successful steam engine

James Watt

Newcomen's 'fire engine' wasted most of the heat in the coal it used. During the next 50 years several engine makers thought of improvements to the design to save fuel. But the really big improvement was made by James Watt.

Watt was a scientific instrument-maker at Glasgow University. During the eight years he worked there (1756–64) he often talked and argued with students and teachers who dropped into his workshop.

At this time Glasgow was the leading university in the world for the study of heat. The thermometer had been invented about a hundred years earlier by Galileo, but the improved thermometer of Gabriel Fahrenheit had only been made in 1714. Much careful work was done at Glasgow in the early eighteenth century. Joseph Black, Professor of Chemistry there was the first person to measure the total amount of heat needed to raise the temperature of various substances, and to turn ice into water, or water into steam. By careful weighing and calculation he laid the basis of the modern science of heat.

Glasgow University had a model of a Newcomen engine. It never seemed to have enough steam to work properly, and in 1763 Watt was asked to mend it. Using Black's methods, he worked out that it used about three times as much steam as was needed. He then conducted a new series of experiments on the temperature and pressure of steam. He saw that the trouble was not a defect in the Glasgow model. It was a basic weakness in Newcomen's design.

Watt spent two years thinking, experimenting and talking. He knew quite well that an answer to this problem would produce a far better steam engine, which was badly needed in mines and ironworks. 'I could think of nothing else but this machine', he wrote to a friend.

The answer came to him in May 1765 as he was walking on Glasgow Green. Why not condense the steam in a separate container and not inside the cylinder? 'I had not walked further than the golf house when the whole thing was arranged in my mind,' he said later.

So far these were just ideas. Watt had to borrow over £1000 from Joseph Black just to go on with his experiments. To make the first scientifically designed engine took him another 11 years and cost many thousands of pounds. Watt's first partner, John Roebuck, went bankrupt, and his second partner, Matthew Boulton, took very great risks though they paid off in the end. One reason why they took such risks is that they both had a good understanding of science.

- *How would this encourage them?*

- *How important was scientific knowledge as a factor making possible the steam engine?*

Newcomen's engine, on the left, wasted most of the heat in the coal it used. Watt's solution was to condense the steam in a separate container, and not inside the cylinder

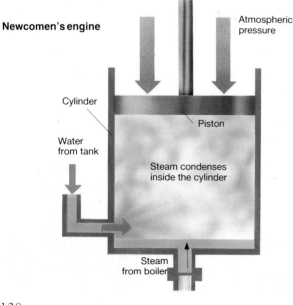

Newcomen's engine

Atmospheric pressure

Cylinder

Piston

Water from tank

Steam condenses inside the cylinder

Steam from boiler

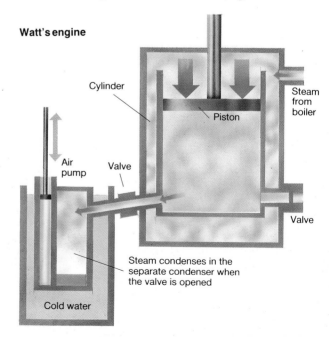

Watt's engine

Cylinder

Steam from boiler

Piston

Air pump

Valve

Valve

Steam condenses in the separate condenser when the valve is opened

Cold water

Science and energy since the steam engine

During the nineteenth and twentieth centuries many new sources of energy were discovered, and many new machines invented to make use of it. You will find plenty of evidence in the narrative of the importance of science in making these developments possible.

Gas

The gas used for lighting was a by-product of coal. But much scientific knowledge was needed to purify it and make gas lighting work.

■ *What does the cartoon on the right show about the public attitude to science in Britain at this time?*

Electricity

Many early machines, like the first steam engine, had been made by practical craftsmen, like Newcomen, who knew very little science. Edison was a practical craftsman, with little formal education. But he knew how important science was.

Source 265 Scientific researches. A cartoon by Gillray, 1802. The Royal Institution was an important centre for research. Sir Humphrey Davy is shown here holding the bellows. He made many important discoveries in chemistry

Oil

Oil has been used since the Stone Age. But before it could become important, geologists had to know where to drill for it and chemists had to refine it. Like the other modern energy industries it depends greatly on science.

Nuclear energy

Source 264 **Edison's research methods**

Edison's laboratory notebooks for 1878 and 1879 suggest the method he used to invent a system of incandescent lighting. His method involved a rational combination of scientific law, economic principles and facts, endless calculations, and tireless experimentation. Able and intelligent assistants such as John Kreusi and Francis Upton followed his leads and also filled the Menlo Park notebooks with drawings, experimental data and calculations using the equations of scientific laws. The notebooks show that they were all informed about earlier generators, arc lights, and other components, especially those of European origin.

(Thomas P. Hughes: *Thomas Edison, Professional Inventor*, 1976)

Source 266 From the *Evening Standard*, 9 August 1945. The figure on the left represents the scientist.

■ *Did the cartoonist think people were likely to use nuclear power wisely?*

"BABY PLAY WITH NICE BALL?"

Old ideas still in use

Source 267 An athlete lighting the Olympic flame at the 1984 Olympic Games, Los Angeles. The flame was carried by relays of athletes from Greece

This section has been mainly about the coming of new ideas about science and machines. But as well as accepting new ideas people often hold on to old ones for a long time.

A few miles away from Glasgow when James Watt was working on his first steam engine, much older ideas were still accepted.

Source 268 **Sacred fires in Scotland**
On the first of May the herdsmen of every village hold their 'Bel-tien', a sacrifice. They make a fire of wood on which they prepare a large pan of eggs, butter, oatmeal and milk. They bring, besides these ingredients plenty of beer and whiskey. The rites begin with the spilling of some of the mixture on the ground. On that everyone takes a cake of oatmeal, upon which are raised knobs. Each person then turns his face to the fire, breaks off a knob and flinging it over his shoulder says. 'I give this to thee, preserve thou my horses; this to thee, preserve thou my sheep'; and so on. When the ceremony is over they dine on the food.
(Thomas Pennant: *Tour in Scotland*, 1771)

Similar fire festivals were held in many other parts of Europe at Midsummer, Hallowe'en (31 October) and Midwinter.

- *What modern custom resembles the one described in source 268?*

- *In what ways is it similar to the sacrifice described in source 256 on page 132?*

- *Why should old ideas like those in the picture on the left last so long?*

Ideas and the history of energy

- *What ideas have been important in the history of energy?*

- *How did ideas slow down change and how did they speed it up?*

- *What changes in the use of energy could not have taken place unless changes had taken place first in people's ideas?*

SOME PROBLEMS IN THE HISTORY OF ENERGY

How did the various factors work together to bring about the events that actually happened? Why did things turn out as they did?

Historians cannot always answer questions like this. Sometimes events seem to have happened by accident. It is like a soccer match – a first division team is likely to beat one from division four, but sometimes the division four side will win. So historians can never explain the events of history with the same certainty as scientists can explain the results of an experiment.

But historians can explain some things. They can often answer questions about why people behaved as they did. They can explain why what happened was more likely to happen than anything else. They can explain why peoples' actions sometimes led to outcomes they didn't expect.

This part of the book asks five questions about the history of energy.

1 Why did change happen rapidly at some times and places and much more slowly at others?

2 What have been the important trends and turning points?

3 Why did important events happen when they did? Could they have happened earlier, or not have happened at all?

4 How important was the part played by particular individuals in causing important changes?

5 Have things got better or worse, or have they stayed much the same?

141

11

The speed of change

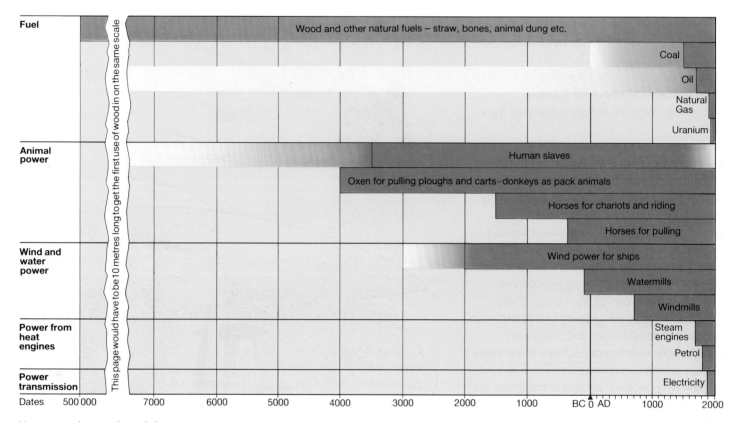

Human use of energy through time

- *Why did change speed up after AD 1000?*
- *Why did it happen in Europe?*
- *Why had it not happened when watermills were first invented?*

Periods of change

Two periods of rapid change are shown on this time-chart. One of them began about 300 years ago and is still going on.

- *How many of the changes shown have happened in the lifetime of an old person still alive today?*

The earlier period of rapid change is not so obvious because it was spread over about 2000 years. This is still 'rapid' compared to the speed at which change happened between 500000 and 4000 BC.

- *Why did the rate of change speed up:*
  a) *c.6000 years ago?*
  b) *c.300 years ago?*
- *Are the reasons the same or different?*

The time chart deals with changes anywhere in the world. If we think only about Europe we can see a third period of rapid change. It began about AD 1000, when Europeans began to build many water-powered machines.

Slow and rapid change

Today people in the rich parts of the world are so used to rapid change that they expect it. But through most of history, things have changed very slowly. Many people in the past saw no important changes throughout their whole lives. Others have seen many changes within their lifetimes.

- *What differences are there between the two carts?*

- *About how many full lifetimes (c. 70 years) were there between the making of the model and the taking of the photograph?*

Source 269 A patent application for a Benz car, 1886

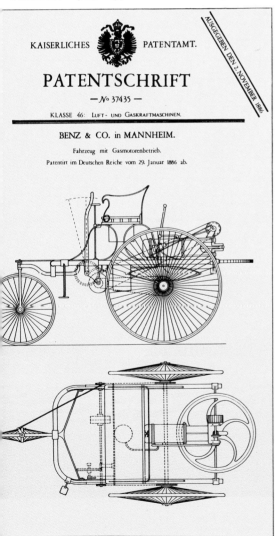

Source 270 This model of a bullock cart was found in Mohenjo Daro, an ancient Indian city. It dates from before 1250 BC

Source 271 A photograph of a bullock cart taken in India, about AD 1930

- *What differences are there between the two cars?*

- *How many lifetimes were there between them?*

- *Why did the design of cars change more quickly than the design of bullock carts?*

A Mercedes-Benz 190 car, 1986

143

Stop-start-stop (intermittent change)

Source 272 Augustin Mouchot's sun-powered steam engine at the Universal Exposition in Paris, 1878. This machine reflected the sun's rays on to the boiler at the centre of the cone. It raised enough steam to work a small engine

Source 273 Sun power plant built in Egypt, by Frank Shuman, 1913. It produced 55 h.p., enough to pump 6000 gallons of water a minute. It cost twice as much to build as a coal-fired steam engine, but since sunlight was free it saved enough to pay off the extra cost in two years

Changes do not always take place at a steady pace. Sometimes things change and develop in fits and starts, stopping and starting again several times.

Power from the sun

Source 274 Reaping the rays of the sun
Eventually industry will no longer find in Europe the resources to satisfy its enormous expansion . . . Coal will undoubtedly be used up. What will industry do then? Reap the rays of the sun!
(A. Mouchot: *Solar Heat* Paris, 1879)

Source 276 Sun power is now a fact
Sun power is now a fact. It will have a history something like aerial navigation. Up to twelve years ago it was a mere possibility and no practical man took it seriously. The Wrights made an 'actual record' flight and thereafter developments were more rapid. We have made an 'actual record' in sun power, and we also hope for quick developments.
(F. Shuman: Scientific American, 1914)

Shuman was wrong. In 1914 the oil industry and the internal combustion engine were developing rapidly. With plenty of cheap oil and small reliable engines it was soon no longer worth-while to build expensive solar powered steam engines. No more were built for a long time. It looked as if the solar powered steam engine was a failure.

- *Why did experiments like the one below begin again in the 1970s? (This is not the only one.)*

- *Can we be sure that the development of solar power will carry on? Might it stop again, as it did after 1913?*

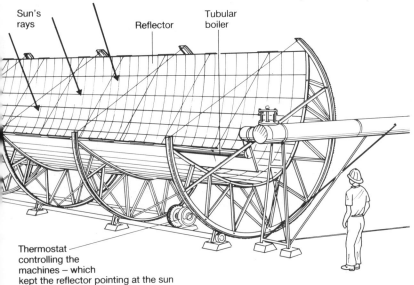

Sun's rays

Reflector

Tubular boiler

Thermostat controlling the machines – which kept the reflector pointing at the sun

Source 275 Experimental solar powered engine in New Mexico, USA, 1977. The engine is of 25 horsepower and pumps 700 gallons of water a minute for irrigation

Dead ends

Pillars of stone or tiles support the floor

Hollow tiles in wall form a chimney

Source 277 A modern reconstruction of a hypocaust, based on archaeological remains

Sometimes changes reach a 'dead end'. They stop and are not taken up again. For instance the 'hypocaust' central heating system was quite common in the homes of wealthy Romans in Britain and other parts of Europe from the first to the fifth century AD. Nothing similar has been built since. Modern central heating is nothing like the Roman hypocaust.

False dawns

Sometimes people have great hopes of new and wonderful sorts of energy that never became possible at all. One such 'false dawn' was the 'perpetual motion machine', a machine that would work for ever without any power to drive it.

It was not until the 1840s that scientists proved that machines of this sort could never work. Perpetual motion machines are impossible.

How can people tell?

We can tell which historical changes were intermittent and which were dead ends or false dawns because we know what happened afterwards. People living at the time are often wrong.

Source 278 Human flight impossible

'When', inquired the friend, 'will you wing your first flight?'

'Just as soon,' replied the flying machine inventor, 'as I can get the laws of gravitation repealed.'
(Joke in *Puck*, American humorous magazine, 19 October 1904)
On 17 December 1903 the Wright brothers had made their first flight.

- *How can people living at the time tell which developments are likely to continue?*

- *Which developments of the present high energy world might turn out to be dead ends or false dawns?*

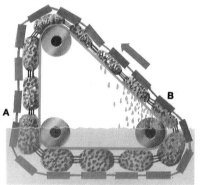

Perpetual motion machine invented by Sir William Congreve FRS (1772–1828). He also invented the first effective European war rockets. As the sponge **A** soaked up water it would become heavier. At the same time the chain pressed on the sponges at **B**, squeezed them out and made them lighter. This, Congreve thought, would make the belt of sponges move

- *Developments often ran into 'dead-ends' because other things changed. What changes put a stop to the two developments above?*

12 Trends and turning points

It is not always easy to say whether a change is a turning point or whether it is part of a trend.

1 A trend takes place over a long time. A turning point takes place rapidly.

2 A trend is a series of events, but a turning point can be just one event.

3 A trend worsens or improves existing things. A turning point may bring into existence something quite new.

A *trend* is a gradual change. After a *turning point* things are quite different in at least one important way. For example moving up from the first year to the fifth year is a 'trend' in your life at school. Leaving school and starting work will be a turning point.

- *What other trends and what turning points are shown in this drawing?*

- *What trends or turning points have taken place in your life up to now?*

Energy use in the kitchen

The development of cooking and the kitchen

1 Hunter-gatherers of the Old Stone Age. A fire drill is lying on the ground

2 Ancient Egypt (from tomb paintings, about 2500 BC). (The object in centre of the bottom row, that looks like a bell, is in fact a fan)

■ *Can you identify the different activities?*

3 Roman Britain, about AD 200 (based on archaeological remains). The pile of spare charcoal can be seen beneath the stove

4 England, 1066 (from the Bayeux Tapestry). The meat is being boiled in a cauldron. But notice the meat on the shelf behind, ready spitted for roasting

147

5 Eighteenth-century England. A tinder box sits next to the candle on the table.

■ *How is the spit powered?*

6 England about 1850. Gas-lighting had recently been introduced

7 A modern kitchen

■ *For what different purposes has energy been used in the kitchen?*

■ *What turning points have there been?*

■ *What trends have there been in its use?*

Asking questions about trends and turning points

Statements about trends and turning points are not 'facts' like dates. They are 'judgements' made by historians about changes and about what part these changes played in the history of energy. They depend on the questions historians ask. For instance, questions might be asked about changes in the sorts of things people used energy for, or in the amounts they used. Each might lead to a different answer about trends and turning points. Other questions could be asked about a) the source of energy used, b) how the energy was harnessed and c) how much was wasted.

Energy to drive machines

Two questions about the changes in the use of energy to drive machines are:

1 What sorts of energy have been used?
2 How much work could machines do?

Measures of power

For most of history people have been content to say 'as strong as an ox' or 'as strong as a horse'. There was no need to measure power exactly. But in 1783 James Watt needed an exact measurement so that he could compare his engines with horses. So he measured exactly how much work a horse could do in a given time. Since then many engines have been measured in 'horse-power'. In 1799 a new system of measurement, the metric system was begun in France. It has since been accepted in all countries. Under this system the unit of power is the watt. A man can produce about 75 watts of power and a horse about 750.

- *What have been the main turning points in the sorts of energy used to drive machines?*

- *What have been the main turning points in the amounts of work that the machines can do?*

- *What have been the main trends?*

Source of power	Date	Power produced in kilowatts	Equivalent in manpower
Man by himself	before 10 000 BC	0.075	1
Ox pulling	before 4000 BC	0.56	7
Donkey working mill	c.300 BC	0.15	2
First water wheel	c.100 BC	2	30
Horizontal windmill	c. AD 800	not known	–
Horse for heavy pulling	c. AD 800	0.75	10
First steam engine	1712	2.3	33
Later windmill	c.1800	10	130
Later steam engine	c.1800	35	466
Later water wheel	1827	175	2300
First water turbine	1833	4.5	60
First internal combustion engine	1860	2.8	37
Largest steam piston engine	1876	1750	23 000
First steam turbine	1884	7.5	100
Modern steam turbine	1976	1.3 million	17.3 million
Modern windmill	1981	2500	33 333
Modern internal combustion engine	1984	28 000	373 000
Modern water turbine	1984	715 000	9.5 million

KEY   Sources of power

Man and animal

Steam engines

Windmills and watermills

Internal combustion engines

The use of fire

Peking Man about 500 000 years ago, used fire to cook, to harden his tools, and to provide warmth and light. This time chart would have to be 45 metres long to include that. It is only able to show when some of the more recent uses were first introduced.

- What different ways of using fire have people developed?

- Did any of these developments mark turning points in the use of fire or were they all part of a gradual trend?

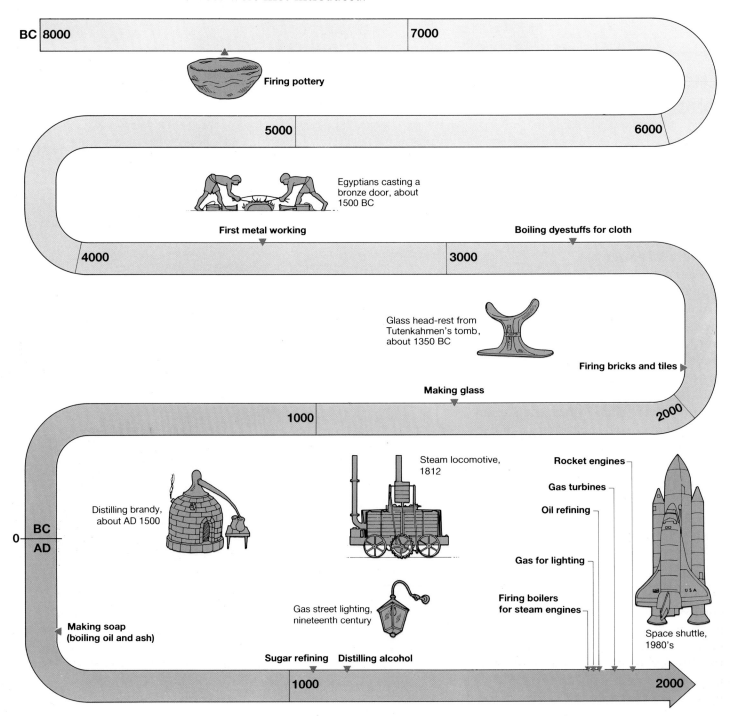

BC 8000

7000

Firing pottery

5000

6000

Egyptians casting a bronze door, about 1500 BC

First metal working

Boiling dyestuffs for cloth

4000

3000

Glass head-rest from Tutenkahmen's tomb, about 1350 BC

Firing bricks and tiles

Making glass

1000

2000

Distilling brandy, about AD 1500

Steam locomotive, 1812

Rocket engines

Gas turbines

Oil refining

0 BC / AD

Gas for lighting

Making soap (boiling oil and ash)

Gas street lighting, nineteenth century

Firing boilers for steam engines

Space shuttle, 1980's

Sugar refining   Distilling alcohol

1000

2000

The development of electricity

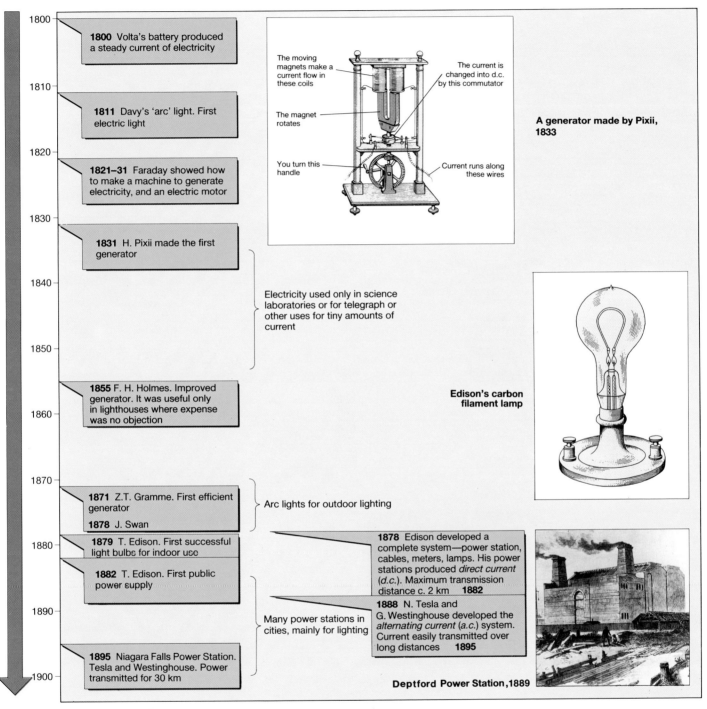

1800

1800 Volta's battery produced a steady current of electricity

1810

1811 Davy's 'arc' light. First electric light

1820

1821–31 Faraday showed how to make a machine to generate electricity, and an electric motor

1830

1831 H. Pixii made the first generator

1840

Electricity used only in science laboratories or for telegraph or other uses for tiny amounts of current

1850

1855 F. H. Holmes. Improved generator. It was useful only in lighthouses where expense was no objection

1860

1870

1871 Z.T. Gramme. First efficient generator

1878 J. Swan

Arc lights for outdoor lighting

1879 T. Edison. First successful light bulbs for indoor use

1880

1882 T. Edison. First public power supply

Many power stations in cities, mainly for lighting

1890

1878 Edison developed a complete system—power station, cables, meters, lamps. His power stations produced *direct current* (*d.c.*). Maximum transmission distance c. 2 km **1882**

1888 N. Tesla and G. Westinghouse developed the *alternating current* (*a.c.*) system. Current easily transmitted over long distances **1895**

1895 Niagara Falls Power Station. Tesla and Westinghouse. Power transmitted for 30 km

1900

The moving magnets make a current flow in these coils

The current is changed into d.c. by this commutator

The magnet rotates

You turn this handle

Current runs along these wires

A generator made by Pixii, 1833

Edison's carbon filament lamp

Deptford Power Station, 1889

Questions can be asked the history of energy as a whole, or about separate parts of it. The coming of electrical power is an important turning point in the history of energy, but there were also turning points in the way it developed in the nineteenth century.

■ *What were the trends or turning points in the history of electricity, 1800–1900?*

■ *Was any of these nineteenth century developments a turning point in the history of energy as a whole?*

The picture of Deptford Power Station shown above comes from the *Illustrated London News*, 26 October 1889. It was the first of the world's big power stations. Its a.c. current was transmitted seven miles to central London at 10,000 volts.

Which changes are important?

Historians try to include important facts and ideas and leave out those that matter less. The difficulty is to tell which are which. This is because changes are important in different ways. For instance the wood shortage in seventeenth century Europe mattered because it affected the lives of many people, but the invention of the rocket engine mattered because it led to other changes, like nuclear missiles or space exploration.

How important were these changes?

- *Did each of these affect the lives of many people or only a few?*

- *Did each make an important difference to people or only a slight one?*

- *Did each change last for a long time or only for a short one?*

- *Was each a turning point, or part of a trend, or neither of these?*

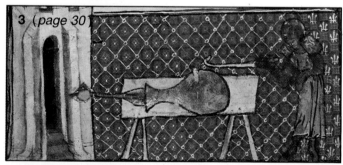

1 (*page 26*)

Top millstone turns

Waterwheel driven by stream

Bottom millstone stays still

Gears to transmit power

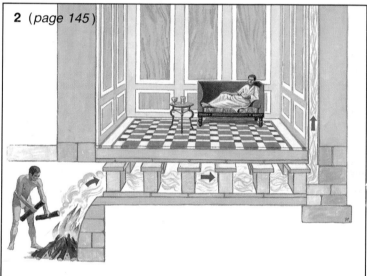

2 (*page 145*)

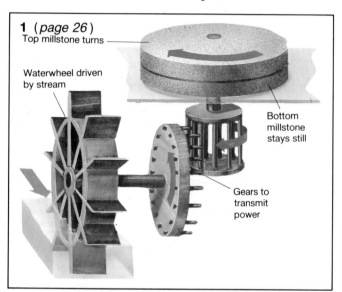

3 (*page 30*)

5 (*page 66*)

4 (*page 34*)

13 Why did it happen then?

Why do things happen in history?

The development of the steam engine was one of the most important changes in the history of energy. Why did it happen in eighteenth century Britain and not at some other time and place?

The answer to this question is complicated, because the actions and ideas of thousands of people were involved. There were also impersonal factors – for instance Britain happened to have a good supply of coal. A way to simplify the question is to break into parts:

1 *Needs*: Why did people in eighteenth century Britain need steam engines? Was there no other way in which they could have solved their problems?

2 *Conditions*: What else was necessary before a steam engine could be made? Some of these conditions were practical, like a good supply of coal. Some were technical skills or scientific knowledge. Some were to do with finance and the attitudes of businessmen.

If you can find evidence to show that there was an urgent need for the steam engine and that the conditions for producing it were all available, you have done as much as is possible to explain its causes.

The invention of the steam engine

To explain the coming of the steam engine in eighteenth century Britain you should ask the following questions:

- *Why was the steam engine needed?*
- *What necessary practical things like coal were available?*
- *What necessary technical skill was available?*
- *What necessary scientific knowledge was available?*
- *What necessary economic and industrial conditions existed?*

Miners needed a better pump

By 1700 Britain was dependent on coal, because supplies of wood and charcoal were scarce. Only in Britain was coal mined in large amounts.

Source 280 The poor can't manage without coal

For several years the price of coal hath been raised and kept up at so exorbitant a degree as to be a very great grievance, especially to those engaged in the several branches of trade. Coal is absolutely necessary to the numerous poor people. They have found the high rise of its price to be an almost unbearable oppression.
(Petition of the inhabitants of Southwark to the House of Commons, 1738)

The deeper the coal mines went, the more serious became the problem of flooding. By 1700 the coal mines in Northumberland were usually more than 35 metres and some as much as 120 metres deep.

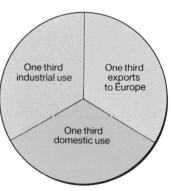

Total production about 3 million tonnes

British coal production and use, about 1700

Conditions that made the steam pump possible

Source 282 An engine to drain mines

Captain Savery's Engine which raises water by the force of fire to any height is now brought to perfection and ready for public use.

All Proprietors of Mines and Collieries which are troubled with water may be provided with Engines to drain the same, at his workhouse at Salisbury Court, London, near the old Playhouse. It may be seen working on Wednesdays and Saturdays every week from 3 to 6 in the afternoon. They may be satisfied that it will do the work with less expense than any other force of Horse or Hands, and less subject to repairs.

(Advertisement in *The Postman*, 1702)

Captain Thomas Savery, who advertised his engine in 1702 (Source 80), was a Fellow of the Royal Society. This had been set up forty years earlier to encourage science.

■ *Was his scientific knowledge likely to help him to design his engine?*

Savery's engine worked partly by condensing steam to make a vacuum. This was something which scientists in the seventeenth century had studied a good deal. In 1600 most scientific thinkers had believed that it was impossible to make a vacuum.

By 1700 they knew that vacuums could be made in various ways, and they understood the great power of atmospheric pressure pushing air or water in to fill one. It was this atmospheric pressure which Savery was using to raise water.

Savery's machine was not very successful. Few were made and none used in mines.

Source 283 Steam blows open the Savery engine

I have known Capt. Savery at York Buildings make steam 8 or 10 times stronger than common air (8–10 times atmospheric pressure) and then its heat was so great that it would melt common soft solder, and its strength so great as to blow open several of the joints of his machine. So he was forced to be at pains and charge to have all his joints soldered with spelter or hard solder.

(J.T. Desaguliers: *Experimental Philosophy*, 1744)

Source 281 From *The Miner's Friend*, a pamphlet by Savery, 1702

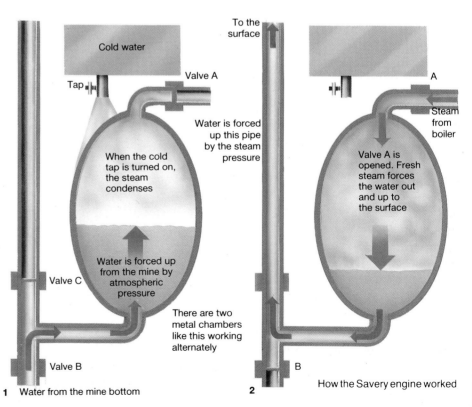

1 Water from the mine bottom

Cold water

Tap

When the cold tap is turned on, the steam condenses

Valve C

Water is forced up from the mine by atmospheric pressure

Valve B

To the surface

Valve A

Water is forced up this pipe by the steam pressure

There are two metal chambers like this working alternately

A

Steam from boiler

Valve A is opened. Fresh steam forces the water out and up to the surface

B

2 How the Savery engine worked

Plate XXXVII.
front. p. 490.

Source 284 The Newcomen engine erected at Oxclose colliery, Durham, 1717. A drawing by Henry Beighton, who erected it

Thomas Newcomen probably knew very little science, but he knew a great deal about mines and pumps. He was a Dartmouth ironmonger who supplied materials to the Cornish tin miners. He must have had a good working knowledge of the pumps in the mines and of the strength of the metals available at the time. He made a much better steam pump. To lift the water, it used an ordinary pump such as had been used in the mines for over a century. The cylinder of the engine in which the steam was condensed, and the piston which moved up and down inside it were also very like parts of the pumps already in use. Like Savery, Newcomen used a vacuum and the pressure of the atmosphere, but he didn't make Savery's mistake of trying to use high pressure steam to push the water up out of the mine. It is likely that this is why he succeeded where Savery had failed. After 1712 Newcomen steam pumps were used in most large coal mines. They were expensive, costing as much as £1500 each, and they wasted most of the coal they burned. But they enabled the mines to go deeper, so more coal could be mined and sold.

- *Why was the first successful steam pump made in Britain in 1712? Why was it needed? What conditions made it possible?*

- *Did Britain need steam pumps more than other countries?*

- *Did Britain have more of the right conditions?*

- *Was it possible for the steam pump to have been invented any earlier?*

155

The development of the rotative steam engine

Thomas Newcomen's 'Fire engine' of 1712 was a steam pump. It could pump water and do nothing else. 75 years later Watt's rotative engine made it possible for steam power to do many other things. So the question, 'why did steam power develop in eighteenth century Britain?' falls into two halves:

- *Why was the steam pump invented in 1712?*

- *Why did people like Watt continue to develop and adapt it for other uses?*

The need for a better steam engine

In the coal mines the wastefulness of the Newcomen engine was not very important. But in other places it was. The Cornish tin miners found that they had to pay high prices for coal. A steam engine that used less of it would be very welcome to them.

All other industries still relied on water-power. As more and more iron was needed, the water-power that worked the bellows and forges ran short.

Source 286 Not enough water-power

12th. June 1733. Ye water is very short which makes ye furnaces go but heavily.

13th. July 1733. Yesterday I was obliged to blow out ye New Furnace, our water being quite gone, but will put in repair both the hearths with the utmost speed against (ready for the time when) water does come.

15th. Nov. 1733. Our water here continues very short. There never was such a complaint at this time of the year. I don't think that there is a forge in ye Country does half work. But there is no remedy but patience.

(Letters from Richard Ford, Manager of the Coalbrookdale Iron works, Shropshire, to T. Goldney, a customer at Bristol)

After about 1760 industry in Britain began to develop more rapidly. It was the cotton industry, using machines powered by hand and by water that grew fastest. But more and more iron was needed too, and a more reliable source of energy than water power was needed at the iron works.

Conditions that made Watt's engine possible

James Watt worked in Glasgow University. Here Professor Joseph Black was at the time making the first accurate measurements ever made of the amounts of heat used for various purposes. Watt made the instruments that Black used for this. He also used to them to measure the amount of heat used by a model of the Newcomen engine. Using Black's scientific ideas, he could see that this wasted a lot of the heat from the steam. He then used his scientific understanding of heat to invent the 'separate condenser', which avoided the waste. This was the most important of Watt's inventions.

Source 287 Wilkinson helps Watt to help Wilkinson

The early cylinders delivered to Watt for his steam-engines were not satisfactory, since they were not sufficiently accurate in bore to prevent leakage of steam. It was John Wilkinson who produced the first completely satisfactory cast iron cylinders for steam-engines by a new method he had invented for boring cannon and patented in 1774. The improvement in the steam-engine was tremendous.

In 1776 a steam-engine was used for the first time for purposes other than for pumping water. This engine was used to blow Wilkinson's furnace at Willey in

Source 285 John Wilkinson's machine to bore cannon or cylinders, 1775. A reconstructed model in the Science Museum, London

Shropshire. Four years later Wilkinson had four engines employed in producing blast for iron-smelting. The success of Watt's invention soon led other ironmasters to order furnace engines.
(H.R. Schubert: *Oxford History of Technology*, 1957)

Source 288 Accurate work
Wilkinson hath bored us several cylinders almost without error; that of fifty inches diameter for Bentley & Co. doth not err the thickness of an old shilling in no part.
(Letter from Boulton to Watt, 1776)

Source 289 A big investment, but worth it
John Roebuck, M.D. said
. . . that £2000 at the least had been expended in bringing the Fire Engines to their present state.
. . . that this engine will not consume half the steam that a common fire engine does, probably not the third part, and produce an equal effect.
. . . that it will at least do double the work of a common fire engine at the same expense.
. . . that it may be applied wherever any kind of mechanical power is wanted.
He is of opinion the money already expended, together with a moderate stock to carry this invention into execution may amount to £10000. An expensive apparatus is necessary for making these engines, particularly boring and turning mills for making of cylinders; and foundries for casting them must be errected, in order to bore the cylinders with sufficient accuracy. These mills will cost a very considerable sum of money.

Matthew Boulton, Esquire, said . . .
. . . A very large sum of money will be required to carry this invention into execution . . .
. . . It is not only the cheapest mechanical power yet invented, except wind and water mills, but it may be applied to an infinite number of purposes to which the common fire engine is not at all applicable.
He had great reason to believe that if this invention was once established into a regular manufactory, great numbers of

engines would be exported to various parts of the European continent.
(Evidence to House of Commons Committee, Commons Journals, 1775)

- *Why was Watt's steam engine developed in later eighteenth century Britain? Why was it needed? What conditions made it possible?*

Hero's 'steam engine', Alexandria, 100 BC
Something rather like a steam engine was invented in Alexandria about 100 BC, but it came to nothing.

This drawing comes from Hero of Alexandria's book 'Pneumatics', written between 100 BC and AD 100. It is from the oldest surviving copy, written in Greek about AD 1500. Hero was one of a group of Greek thinkers working at Alexandria between 300 BC and AD 100. His book mentions many other machines that used heat to do mechanical work, like opening the doors of a temple or making figures move on an altar. We know that there were many copies of his work in Greek and Roman times, but nobody took up his idea of using the power of steam to move things.

- *Why was a steam engine not developed following the work of Hero of Alexandria?*

- *What needs for power were there at the time? How were they met?*

- *Were any of the conditions for a successful steam engine present at the time?*

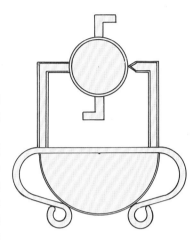

Source 290 *Above*: A copy of the Greek drawing, about AD 1500 and *Below*: How Hero's engine worked

157

14 People and energy

In the history of energy the story has mainly been about the coming of new machines like water mills and steam engines, or new fuels like coal and uranium. What about the people?

How important were they in bringing about change? What part was played by individual inventors or thinkers or business men? Were the changes bound to happen anyhow even if particular people had never lived?

To decide how much difference someone made to the history of energy you should ask:

a) What change were they connected with?

b) How important was this change?

c) What did the person learn from other people?

d) What did they discover or do for themselves?

e) Were other people trying to do the same thing?

f) Is it likely that someone else might have succeeded?

Abraham Darby I, 1678–1717

Darby's early life

Abraham Darby was born in 1678 near Dudley in Warwickshire. The area was famous for iron-working. In hundreds of small back-yard workshops people made nails and other small items of hardware. Abraham's father was both a farmer and a nail-maker, and Abraham must have learned about iron-working as soon as he was able to watch and help in the workshop. His father was rich enough to send him to school and when he was 14 to pay the fee to apprentice him to a Birmingham mill-wright, Jonathan Freeth. Freeth made mills for grinding malt for the brewers. It was in his workshop that Abraham learned how to make cast iron, which was used to make parts for the malt mills.

At this time the shortage of wood to make charcoal for the iron industry was very serious. There was plenty of coal in Warwickshire and in nearby counties like Staffordshire and Shropshire, but all attempts to use it in blast furnaces and refining furnaces had failed.

Source 291 Dud Dudley: inventor or liar?

Wood and charcoal growing then scant and pit coles abounding near the furnace did induce me to alter my furnace and to attempt by my new invention the making of iron with pit cole . . . After I had made a second blast and trial I found the quality to be good and profitable, but the quantity did not exceed three tons a week.
(D. Dudley: *Metallum Martis or Iron made with Pitcole, Seacole, etc.* 1665)

In 1619 Dudley was manager of his father's ironworks in Warwickshire.

Dudley took out a patent for his process in 1621, but neither the patent nor his book give any details of what the process was. He claimed that he could make iron for £4 a ton and sell it for £12. Apart from his own book there is no other evidence of his success.

Source 292 Coke used by the brewers

This country (Staffordshire) could not well subsist without vast supplies of coal, the wood being most of it spent upon the iron works. Coal is now used in all the mechanical works that require great expense of fuel except the iron works. For malting they have a way of charring the coal the same as they do wood. By this the coal is freed from those noxious steames that would otherwise give the malt an ill odour. The coal thus prepared they call coakes, which gives almost as strong a heat as charcoal itself and is as fit for most other uses except for the smelting fixing or refining of iron. This it cannot be brought to do, though attempted by the most skilful artists.

(Robert Plot: *History of Staffordshire* Oxford, 1686)

■ *Was Abraham Darby likely to know about Dud Dudley or about the brewer's use of coke?*

Darby's first new idea: cast iron pots

When Darby finished his apprenticeship in 1699, he married a Dudley girl, Mary Sergeant, and moved with his young wife to Bristol. Here he joined a partnership making iron and brass goods. He was interested in new methods and the firm was rich enough to try them out. In 1704 Darby brought some Dutch craftsmen to Bristol. With their help Darby and his partners began to make cast brass cooking pots. Brass was an expensive metal, but it was the only one that could be used to make pots. The result was that only rich people could buy them. If iron could be used instead, pots could be made far cheaper, and far more people would be able to afford them.

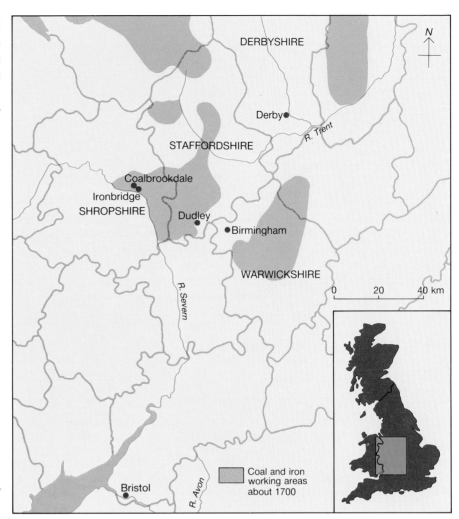

This map shows the location of Coalbrookdale

Source 293 Darby's patent for iron pots

A new way of casting iron bellied potts and other iron bellied ware . . . by which iron potts and other ware may be cast fine and with more ease and may be afforded cheaper than they can be by the way commonly used, and in regard to their cheapness may be if great use to the poor of this Kingdom. (Patent issued to Darby 1707.)

In 1708 Darby made a big decision. He moved from Bristol to Coalbrookdale in Shropshire. Here he rented a disused blast furnace where he could specialise in iron pots and build up a new business. It had excellent transport to Bristol on the river Severn, and was only a day's ride from his old home near Dudley. There was still woodland in the area where charcoal could be made for the furnaces. But the price of charcoal was rising all the time.

Source 294 Cooking pots manufactured at the Darby works in Coalbrookdale, in the Ironbridge Gorge Museum

Darby uses coke instead of charcoal

Near Coalbrookdale there was plenty of cheap coal. Some of this was similar to the coal used by the brewers to make coke. Soon after coming to Coalbrookdale Darby tried it in his blast furnace instead of charcoal.

Source 296 Abraham Darby uses coke to make iron

It was my husband's father, Abraham Darby that attempted to mould cast iron pots etc., in which he succeeded. About the year 1709 he came into Shropshire to Coalbrookdale and with other partners took a lease of the works which consisted only of an old blast furnace and some forges. Here he cast iron goods out of the blast furnace that blowed with wood charcoal, for it was not then thought of to blow with pit coal. Some time after he suggested the thought that it might be practicable to smelt the iron from the ore in the blast furnace with pit coal. Upon this he first tried it with raw coal as it came out of the mines, but it did not answer. He, not discouraged, had the coal coak'd into cynder as is done for drying malt and it then succeeded to his satisfaction. But he found only one sort of pit coal which would suit best for the making of good iron . . . He then erected another blast furnace and enlarged the works. This discovery soon got abroad and became of great utility.

(Letter written about 1775 by Abiah Darby, wife of Abraham's son, Abraham Darby II. Abraham I died in 1717.)

It is clear from the account books at Coalbrookdale that coke was being made and used by 1711. The new furnace mentioned by Abiah was built in 1715.

Darby's process would only work for making cast iron. To make other sorts of iron a better bellows and a hotter furnace were needed. So the real growth of the iron industry could not begin for another 40 or 50 years. In 1711 coke could only be used by someone who wanted a lot of cheap cast iron – for things like cooking pots.

- *Would other people have soon made the discovery even without Darby? Or was Darby unusually clever or lucky?*

Cast iron and the steam engine

Abraham Darby I was thinking only of using cast iron for cooking pots. But at almost exactly the same time as he began to use coke, Thomas Newcomen was making his first steam engines. Each engine needed a large cylinder, at first made from brass. It was quite simple to adapt the foundry at Coalbrookdale to make cast iron cylinders as well as pots. They were much cheaper than brass ones, and could be made much larger. The first steam engine cylinder was cast at Coalbrookdale in 1722. For many years this was the only place in the world where they could be made. Nearly all the cylinders for Watt's engines were cast there. So the coming of the steam engine was greatly influenced by Darby's invention.

- *How important was Abraham Darby I's work:*
  a) *for the iron industry*
  b) *for the steam engine*
  c) *for the history of energy?*

- *Would things have been much the same if he had never lived?*

Source 295 A furnace from Coalbrookdale, now in the Ironbridge Gorge Museum.

Matthew Boulton, 1728–1809

Matthew Boulton was Watt's partner in developing the steam engine. We should ask ourselves the following questions.

a) What was Boulton's personal contribution?

b) How important was it?

c) Could Watt have made the steam engine without him?

Boulton's family business

Boulton's father was a Birmingham manufacturer of metal buckles and brooches. Matthew went into the family business at the age of fourteen, and by the time he was forty he had built it up into the country's leading factory for ornamental metalwork. He had the best craftsmen and equipment that could be got. He sold his products all over Europe.

Money to invest

Boulton's success was partly because he had money to invest in the business. In 1756 he married his first wife Mary, who had inherited £14000. In 1769 Mary died and Boulton married her sister Anne, who had another £14000. He used this money to build a new factory at Soho, Birmingham in 1761, and later to invest heavily in the steam engine.

Money then and now. A worker who earned 7 shillings (35p) a week in the late eighteenth century might earn £100 a week in the 1980s.

Scientific knowledge

Boulton was not just a rich business-man. He was very interested in art and science. He enjoyed good company, and the talk around his dinner table was often about the latest scientific developments. One of his friends was Benjamin Franklin, inventor and scientist. Another was Joseph Priestley, who discovered oxygen. Boulton and his friends would have had no difficulty in understanding Watt's ideas.

■ *What can we tell from the picture about the interest in science at the time?*

Source 297 Silver candelabrum made for King George III at Boulton's factory, 1770

Source 298 'An experiment on a bird in an air pump', painted in 1768 by Joseph Wright of Derby. This painting shows a well-to-do family like the Boultons. Wright knew Boulton quite well

Not enough power at Soho

Some of the machinery at Soho was driven by a water wheel but the water supply was poor. So in the late 1760s Boulton was thinking about putting in a steam pump. His idea was to pump the water back above the wheel so that the same water could be used again and again. It is typical of Boulton that he designed the machine himself and showed plans to his friends.

Boulton meets Watt

Meanwhile in Scotland, Watt had worked out the main lines of his improved steam engine and gone into partnership with Dr John Roebuck. Roebuck was owner of the best iron-works in Scotland, at Carron near Stirling. He knew Boulton well and wrote to tell him about Watt's ideas. So when in 1768 Watt came to London to get a patent for the engine, he called in at Soho to see Boulton, to admire his factory and to talk about steam engines.

Boulton was so impressed by Watt and his ideas that he offered to make the engines at Soho. This was the suggestion that Watt took back to Roebuck in Scotland.

Boulton's idea was to build a steam engine to pump the water back up from below the wheel

Roebuck would not agree. He would only allow Boulton to make a limited number of engines for local sale near Birmingham. Boulton refused this offer. As he explained to Watt, it was not worth his while.

Source 299 Not worth my while

The plan (making for local sale only) is so different that I cannot agree.

I was excited by two motives to offer you my assistance, which were love of you and love of a money-getting ingenious project. I presume that your engine would require money, very accurate workmanship and extensive correspondence (with customers) to make it turn out to the best advantage. The best means of doing the invention justice would be to keep the work out of the hands of the multitude of practical engineers who from ignorance would affect the reputation of the invention. To remedy this and produce the most profit, my idea was to settle a manufactory near my own by the side of our canal where I would erect all the conveniences necessary for the completion of engines. From this manufactory we would serve all the world with engines of all sizes. By these means and your assistance we could engage and instruct some excellent workmen with more excellent tools than it would be worth any man's while to procure for one single engine. We could execute the invention 20 per cent cheaper than otherwise and with as great a difference in accuracy as there is between the blacksmith and the mathematical instrument maker.

It would not be worth my while to make for three counties only (near Birmingham). But I find it well worth my while to make for all the world.

Nevertheless nothing will alter my inclination to render you all the services in my power. Although there seems to be some obstruction to our partnership in the engine trade, yet I live in hope that you or I may hit on some scheme or other that may associate us.

(Letter from Boulton to Watt, 1769)

■ *Why was Boulton so keen to help?*

Matthew Boulton takes over

By 1773 Watt had still not made his engine work. Then Roebuck went bankrupt. At the same time Watt's wife died, leaving him with two small children, the elder only six. He was in despair.

He was saved by Boulton. Roebuck owned Boulton £1 200, and Boulton agreed to take over Roebuck's share of the engine as payment. Watt moved to Birmingham with his children and the engine. By November 1774 he had it working for the first time.

Boulton and Watt become partners, 1775

Boulton borrows money

For nearly ten years from 1773, Boulton and Watt spent more than they made on the new engines. The result was that, in spite of Boulton's wealth, the firm was short of money and had to borrow. Boulton borrowed £17 000 from London banks. He was full of confidence that the money could be paid back. Watt was a naturally gloomy man and worried a lot about the money. It was 1784 before the firm was out of debt. But Boulton's confidence was fully justified. When he died in 1809 he left a fortune of £150 000, which is equal to several millions in modern money.

Boulton presses for the rotative engine

Until 1783 none of Watt's engines could turn wheels. They were simple steam pumps. The rotative engines made after 1783 made steam power available to drive mills and to turn wheels. The industrial cities of the nineteenth century would have been impossible without it.

Source 300 People want steam powered factories

The people in London, Manchester and Birmingham are steam mill mad. I don't mean to hurry you but I think that . . . we should (decide) to take out a patent for certain methods of procuring rotative motion from the fire engine . . . There is no other Cornwall to be found (Boulton and Watt were at this time making most of their profits from the Cornish tin mines.) The most likely line for the employment of our engine is the application of it to mills, which is certainly an extensive field.

(Letter from Boulton to Watt, January 1781)

Source 301 A steam engine in a brewery, from Rees' *Cyclopaedia*, 1819. The horse wheel was for use if the steam engine broke down. Notice how many machines were driven by one source of power

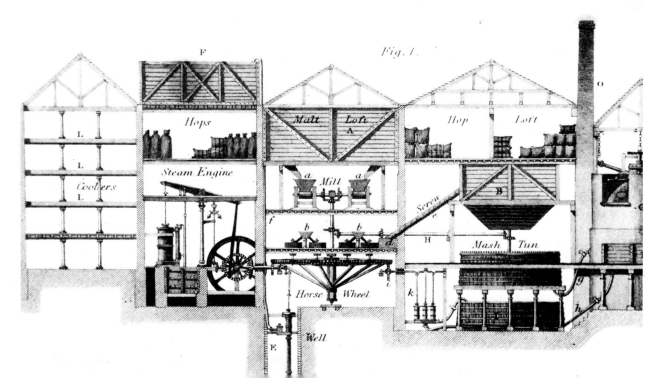

Source 302 Mill engines will not pay

There is no doubt that fire engines will drive mills, but I entertain some doubt whether anything is to be got by this. By the computation I have made of the mill for Reynolds I can't make the profit come to more than £20 a year. It will do little more than pay the trouble.
(Letter from Watt to Boulton, November 1782)

Source 303 There are far more mills than mines

You seem fearful that mills will not (pay) . . . For my part I think that mills though trifles in comparison with Cornish engines, present a field that is boundless and that will be more permanent than these transient mines.
(Letter from Boulton to Watt, December 1782)

Source 304 Don't take any more orders for rotative engines

Every rotative engine will cost twice the trouble of one for raising water and will in general pay only half the money. Therefore I beg of you not to undertake any more rotatives till our hands are clear.
(Letter from Watt to Boulton, January 1784)

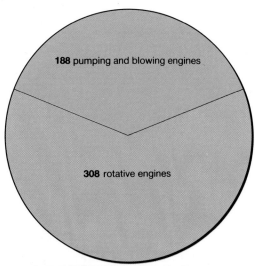

Boulton and Watt engines in use in 1800

■ *Watt designed every one of these engines, and made many important inventions to improve them. How important was the part that Boulton played in this development?*

Source 305 Watt's opinion of Boulton

Mr Boulton was . . . an ingenious mechanic, well skilled in all the practices of the Birmingham manufacturers. He also possessed in a high degree the ability to make any new invention of his own or others useful to the public by organising and arranging the processes whereby it could be carried on. (He also had the ability to) promote the sale by his own exertions and by his numerous friends and correspondents.

His concept of the nature of any invention was quick. He was not less quick in perceiving the uses to which it might be applied and the profits which might accrue from it.

Mr Boulton's active and hopeful disposition served to counterbalance the despondency and diffidence which were natural to me. Mr. Boulton's amiable and friendly character together with his fame as an ingenious and active manufacturer procured me many very active friends in both Houses of Parliament (during arguments about the patents).

The public is indebted for the great benefits they now derive from the machine to his generosity, to the active part he took in the management of the business and to his judicious advice. Without him, or some similar patron (could such a one have been found) the invention could never have been carried out in the length of time it has.
(James Watt, writing just after Boulton's death, 1809)

■ *What part was played by Boulton in developing:*
   a) Watt's first steam engine;
   b) The rotative engine?

■ *How important was the part played by Boulton? Could Watt have succeeded without him?*

Thomas A. Edison, 1847–1931

Thomas Edison was mainly self-educated. His mother quarrelled with his teacher, took him away from school at the age of ten, and taught him herself. When he was twelve he got a job selling papers on the railway. At this time the US railway system was expanding rapidly, and with it the electric telegraph. At 15 Edison became a telegraph operator, and gained from this a thorough practical knowledge of electricity. But he also went on studying by himself, reading Faraday's books and trying to repeat his experiments.

At the age of 22 he invented an improved printing telegraph for the New York Stock Exchange, and was paid $40000 for it. He used the money from this and other inventions to set up an industrial research laboratory, probably the first in the world, at Menlo Park, near New York.

The wizard of Menlo Park

In 1878 Edison was the most famous living inventor. His phonograph – a machine that could talk – seemed like magic. He had made great improvements in the telegraph and the telephone. At 31 he had made a fortune for himself and for the business men he worked with.

Edison's team of scientists and craftsmen were nearly as excited as he was himself by the work they were doing. He made all the main decisions himself. He worked enormously long hours and persuaded his team to do the same. He also had excellent contacts in the world of business and finance. He understood clearly that succesful inventions had to be sold.

Source 306 An inventor, not a scientist
Well I'm not a scientist. I'm an inventor. Faraday was a scientist. He didn't work for money – said he hadn't time to do so. But I

do. I measure everything by the size of the silver dollar. If it doesn't measure up to that standard I know it's no good. (Edison, 1888)

Electric light in 1878

By the later 1870s electric arc lights were in use out of doors. Reliable generators were available to produce the current. It seemed to Edison and to many other people that indoor electric lighting was the next step forward.

Source 307 I believe I can catch up
'I have let the other inventors get the start of me in this matter somewhat, because I have not given much attention to electric light, but I believe I can catch up to them now. Now that I have a machine to make the electricity, I can experiment as much as I please.'

'I think,' he added smiling, 'this is where I can beat the other inventors, as I have so many facilities here for trying experiments.'

'If you make electricity supply the place of gas, you can easily make a great fortune,' the reporter suggested.

'I don't care so much for a fortune,' Mr. Edison replied, 'as I do for getting ahead of the other fellows.'
(*New York Tribune*, 1878)

Source 308 Edison aged 16

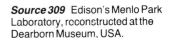

Source 309 Edison's Menlo Park Laboratory, reconstructed at the Dearborn Museum, USA.

Source 310 The generator at Edison's Pearl Street Power Station, New York, 1880s. A contemporary drawing

The light bulb

The problem of making an effective electric light bulb was solved by Swan and Lane-Fox in Britain and by Edison in America at about the same time.

It was in October 1879 that Edison's team made their first successful bulb. In 1880 he set up a special factory to make them, and before the year was out he was selling them even in Britain. Swan had not patented his system because most of the ideas in it were not new. But Edison patented everything. So in most countries for some years the Edison bulbs were the only ones people could buy. In Britain Swan and Edison agreed to set up a joint company to make bulbs.

An electricity distribution system

To Edison the bulb was only a tiny part of a whole system. If electricity was to take the place of gas, dozens of other inventions would be needed.

He began by studying all the problems of making, distributing and selling electricity for lighting part of a city. He sent men to walk the New York streets every hour and record when people lit their gas lights and turned them off. From this his team worked out the total amount of power needed in a city area. Each part of the system, from the generators at the power station to the cables in the streets and the switches and lamps in the houses was then designed to fit together. They decided, for instance, that the electrical pressure

in the system would be 110 volts. This meant that the filaments in the lamps would have to be .38mm. in diameter. The scientists and craftsmen at Menlo Park then set to work to design all the necessary parts of the whole system. In 1880–82 Edison applied for 216 patents.

Edison the businessman

At the same time, Edison and his friends set up several companies to make and sell the equipment. They also set up the Edison Electric Light Company to run the system, and persuaded the cities of London and New York to allow them to dig up the streets to lay the cables.

On 12 January 1882 the first Edison power station was opened at Holborn Viaduct in London. In September 1882 the second one started in New York. It was a remarkable achievement.

How successful was he?

Edison's public distribution system was the first in the world. But it was not very successful. Electric light was more expensive than gas for another thirty years. Some of the early power stations, like the one in London, were closed after a few years. In Europe other inventors and engineers developed their own systems, though often using Edison bulbs.

The complete Edison system was successful only in America. Most of America still uses 110 volts today because of Edison's work. But even in the USA electric light was for a long time an expensive luxury for rich people. Edison companies were not making much profit, and he began to lose interest. In the later 1880s he began to work instead on the gramophone and on motion pictures.

The battle of the systems

Edison's direct current system could only transmit electricity for about two kilometres. During the 1880s Tesla, Westinghouse and other engineers developed the alternating current system, which made possible large power stations and long distance transmission. Edison fought hard against this. He and his friends tried to get laws passed against the use of a.c. on the grounds that it was dangerous. But by the early 1890s they could see that they had failed, and a.c. was beginning to spread. In any case Edison was already interested in other new developments, such as motion pictures, so in 1892 he sold all his shares in the electrical companies he had founded to raise money for his other inventions. After that he took no further part in the development of electric lighting or the supply of electricity, although the 'Edison' companies went on using his name. They still do.

- *Did Edison 'Get ahead of the other fellow'; **a)** with the light bulb? **b)** with the public distribution system?*

- *What did Edison learn from other people?*

- *What did he do himself for the first time?*

- *How important was Edison's contribution to the coming of electic light?*

- *Would it have happened just the same without him?*

'The Greatest Living American'

Edison with the help of his research team made other important inventions. He made the first effective motion picture camera in 1891, and a much improved battery to store electricity in

1909. He greatly improved his earlier invention, the gramophone. Some of his ideas were unsuccessful – for instance he lost several million dollars on a plan to separate iron ore using electro-magnets. But other ideas were successful, and he remained rich and famous.

In the early twentieth century the USA was just becoming a rich and successful world power. Americans were proud of the achievement of their own self-made men. In the 1920s Edison was often described as 'the greatest living American'.

Source 311

The United States takes pride in the thought that his rise from humble beginnings and his unceasing struggle to overcome the obstacles on the road to success well illustrate the spirit of our country.
(President of the USA, C. Coolidge, 'Address in Honour of Mr. Edison'. 1928)

Source 312

I call him the greatest, not merely because of his thousand-odd inventions, nor because of the incredible changes his genius wrought in our civilisation, but because of the exceptional qualities of his human character. He combined the highest characteristics of his nation with intense devotion to the labour of turning ideas and theories into the practicable and the useful.
(*The American Magazine*. December 1931, one month after Edison's death)

- *Why did the photographer decide to take this picture?*

- *Was Edison's reputation in later life justified by his achievements as an inventor and engineer?*

- *What other explanation might there be for this high reputation?*

Source 313 Edison on his 74th birthday in 1921 punching the time clock, like any other worker in his laboratory.

15 Progress: do things improve?

Much of the history of energy through time has been about things getting better. For instance the new horse harness which came into use about AD 900 was better than the old one which tended to throttle the horse. Another example is the power of prime movers. From the early use of animals to the modern use of massive steam turbines, there has been a steady rise in power output.

From examples like this it might look as if history is simply a story of improvements. The idea of steady improvement has been summed up in the word 'progress'. But the history of energy is only one strand in history as a whole.

Suppose you were studying the history of sculpture. It would be hard to argue that the ancient Chinese sculpture (Source 314) is not as good as the modern one (Source 315). So it is not the case that because machines have improved so has everything else.

Some improved machines have had harmful effects as well as good ones. In solving old problems, people have sometimes made new ones that were just as unpleasant.

Source 314 A bronze horse from a Chinese tomb, made about AD 100

Source 315 A bronze horse made by the sculptor Marino Marini, AD 1949

Asking questions about progress 1

■ *What evidence is there in the history of energy which fits in with any of these ideas?*

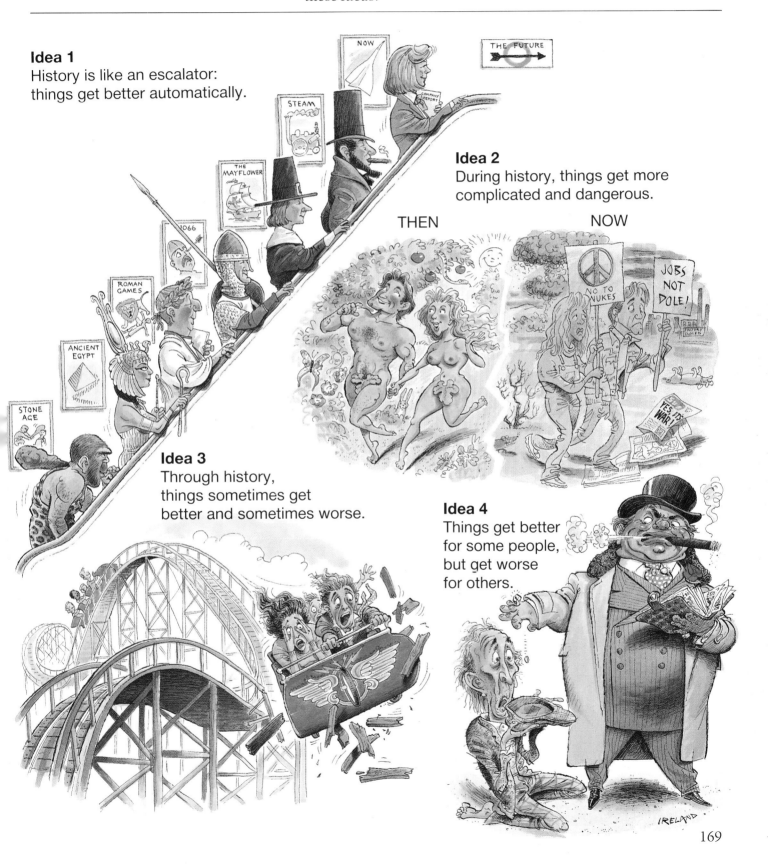

Idea 1
History is like an escalator: things get better automatically.

Idea 2
During history, things get more complicated and dangerous.

THEN

NOW

Idea 3
Through history, things sometimes get better and sometimes worse.

Idea 4
Things get better for some people, but get worse for others.

Asking questions about progress 2

By 'progress' we mean changes that make things steadily better. But changes may make things better in one way and worse in another. For instance, historians might find evidence to support the following opposite opinions.

The writer of the following passage had no doubt that the steam engine was an improvement.

Source 316 One man can do 120 men's work

Steam power now enables a man to do as much work as 120 could do 50 years ago. One bushel of coal, value 3d. (1.5p) will raise 20 000 gallons (9000 litres) of water from a depth of 350 ft. (106m) in a few minutes. This would take 20 men 10 hours to raise with a pump at a cost of £2. Steam does for £1 what would cost £160 by hand. (*The Quarterly Review*, 1826)

- *What arguments might other people in 1826 have put that the steam engine was a change for the worse?*

- *The opposite of progress is regress – things getting steadily worse instead of steadily better. What questions should we ask when deciding whether a change was progress or regress?*

- *If a change seems to have had both good and bad effects how can an historian decide whether it is an example of progress or regress?*

Index

If an entry is in bold print, there is a picture, map or chart referring to the subject on that page. There may also be other references to it in the text on the same page.